THE

SPIRIT

AND

PRESENCE

OF

CHRIST

Wondrous Gifts for the Father's Pleasure

Jerald R. White, Jr.

PRESS

Jan. 21, 2010

Kevin,

Several years ago a copy of this book was given to me. It put me back on the path to pursueing a greater understanding for my pilgrims progress. May you be richly blessed by the gift of both this book and the Holy Spirit.

Mark 13:11 "... for it is not you that speak but the Holy Ghost."

Luke 11:13 "... how much more shall your heavenly Father give the Holy Spirit..."

Acts 2:38 "... and you shall receive the gift of the Holy Ghost."

Ephesians 4:30 "And grieve not the Holy Spirit of God..."

I Thessalonians 5:19 "Quench not the Spirit."

Titus 3:5 "... renewing of the Holy Ghost."

Jesus declared that it is expedient that he should depart so that the Comforter will come. Read John chapters 14-17, noting John 14:16-17, 26; 15:26; 16: 7, 13.

Because Jesus Lives,

Ken

To my family,
and
younger brothers in the faith
whom I have mentored.
You inspire me
and cause me to praise God.
I am thankful!

Contents

Preface ix

Introduction xv

1. Searching for Fullness 19

2. Another Helper Like Jesus 39

3. The Spirit Comes in Fullness 57

4. The Way to Receive Fullness 75

5. The Way to Continue in Fullness 93

6. In Step with the Spirit 115

7. Exceptional Fillings by the Spirit 133

8. Jesus' Presence Revealed 153

9. The Power of Jesus' Presence 175

Conclusion 197

Study Guide 217

For Further Reading 235

Preface

This book is the fruit of a series of messages I gave in Kyoto, Japan, in January 2001. Peter Blocksom of International Chapel Ministries (ICM) heard me do a series on the Holy Spirit at The Evangelical Institute of Greenville in South Carolina during a summer conference in 2000. Afterwards, he asked if I would come to Japan to speak on the same subject in a seminar for missionaries, Japanese Christians, and pastors at International Chapel Ministries. ICM is an umbrella organization in Japan consisting of Christian churches, an elementary school, a secondary school, and an institution of higher education. ICM's mission is to impact Japanese culture with the gospel of Christ.

The messages I delivered in Japan were not intended to be an exhaustive treatment of the subject of the Holy Spirit, but rather an introduction to the reality of the Spirit's presence and His potential fullness for every believer. My aim was to be as biblically accurate as I could be and to make the concepts as simple as possible. We had a limited number of sessions during the first week of January, a Japanese holiday week, and each sentence spoken in English had to be translated into Japanese. This process limited how much I could cover.

I never considered putting these messages into a book because there are so many excellent books on the Holy Spirit by godly men. However, because of what occurred during those days in Japan, Peter

Blocksom requested permission to publish the messages in book form in both Japanese and English. Therefore, the spoken messages have been edited for this book. This means that the material has been rearranged to facilitate reading and that some material has been added to further explain what was spoken. The basic outline of the spoken messages remains the same.

The Holy Spirit significantly revealed Jesus' presence during those days in January 2001. There was conviction of sin with many tears; in fact, I have never seen so many tears in one week's time. Jesus Christ's presence was powerfully real and emphasized with a strong sense of God's love. After the end of several sessions, people just sat in silence for long periods of time, some crying and some praying. At times men wept out loud. Often, as people heard the Scriptures explained, they would wipe their eyes with cloths they had begun to bring to the sessions because they were moved to tears so often by God's Spirit and truths. For the last session, some requested the opportunity to confess their sins publicly, which is most unusual for this culture. About seventy-five people confessed their sins before the group with transparent honesty for two hours, and then the whole group worshiped and praised God for another two hours. The singing came from deep within and had the breath of heaven upon it. The Lord graciously illustrated in experience what the Scriptures were showing us about the Holy Spirit.

Peter Blocksom, who invited me, writes about these sessions in Japan:

> I met Jerry at a conference in South Carolina [during the summer of 2000]. He spoke on the Holy Spirit there, and I saw the Holy Spirit work.
>
> I convinced our pastoral staff [at ICM] to invite him to Japan to minister to our churches. Before delivering his first sermon, I cautioned Jerry by saying, "We are not a Baptist church. We don't give altar calls; people do not go forward for prayer; people do not kneel to pray. So don't ask them to do things like that." After all, these are conservative, reserved Japanese folk who do not show emotion easily.

By the second night, the Spirit of God obviously was moving in our midst. I told Jerry, "Disregard what I told you. Do whatever you feel the Spirit of God leading you to do."

In attendance were not only our church members and missionaries but also some other local pastors, both Weslyan and Baptist, probably totaling eighty to one hundred people (towards the end of the seminar series there were well over one hundred.) Jerry did not tell tear-jerking stories and did not prey upon our emotions as some do, but night after night the Spirit of God poured forth, manifested in many by weeping, by public repentance of sin, and by restoration of relationships. Some, while in silent prayer, felt demons leave their physical being. Japanese men, who seldom show their emotion, cried unashamedly, some on their knees, some standing in adoration— for the presence of God was in our midst. One local pastor wept for forty-five minutes one night during and after the service—on his way to leave, his face was glowing. As he shook my hand and thanked me for inviting him, he commented, "I was in the presence of God."

I am profoundly grateful to our Lord for allowing my wife Gerrie and me to be witnesses to God beautifully working in the hearts of those dear people in Japan whom we came to love so much.

In this book there will be a number of testimonies from individuals who were present when the Holy Spirit manifested the presence of Jesus. These span many years. These experiences occurred in different ways with various kinds of groups. Each time, the Spirit's manifestation came as a surprise, quite unexpectedly, and could not have been predicted. It was always humbling, convicting, and refreshing. Although no human cause or reason could be found that would explain such a profound event, the one consistent human ingredient was heartfelt need expressed through a sincere calling on God. Heaven answered and breathed upon us. However, there have been other times when the prayer was as deep and sincere, but God chose not to reveal His presence in such a significant way. There is always a mystery about God's sovereignty. We diligently seek, but God chooses to answer according to His own perfect wisdom. When God answers so visibly, it is much like the manifestation of His power evident in the healing of the crippled man at the gate called Beautiful. In response to this healing, Peter rebuked the Jewish onlookers for attributing the healing to human sources: "Men of Israel, why are you amazed at this, or why do you gaze at us, as if by our own power or piety we had made him walk? . . . On the basis of faith in His name, it is the name of Jesus which has strengthened this man whom you see and know; and the faith which comes through Him has given him this perfect health in the presence of you all" (Acts 3:12, 16). The power of the Lord and the manifestations of His Spirit are both causes for wonder and amazement.

As you read the eyewitness accounts recorded in these pages, please keep in mind that all glory and praise belong to God alone. These kinds of encounters with God's revealed presence are His sovereign work by the Person of the Holy Spirit. No flesh can cause it to happen. It is not because of the merit of any man or woman. It is entirely and solely the work of God according to His own gracious choosing. All that is required of God's servants is to be cleansed before Him, to be wholly yielded to Him, to pray with faith, to listen and wait for His guidance, and to do as His Spirit leads. The rest is up to Him.

I am grieved to see many Christians not living in the fullness of the Spirit, which God has provided for every believer. Some do not because of ignorance. They just do not know that fullness is possible for them. Others do not enjoy this fullness because they tolerate sin in their lives or because they have not abandoned themselves to Jesus Christ to do His will no matter what the cost. Others are afraid because of foolish excesses they have heard about, or read about, or seen. Some think this fullness of the Holy Spirit is for special servants, but not for them. Others may think that it is only for those who have reached a certain level of maturity. Regardless of the reason, any cause for not living in God's fullness robs the believer of his spiritual birthright purchased by Jesus Christ at the cross. The heavenly Father wants to saturate every believer with His personal presence and power. A Christian life not filled with the Holy Spirit not only robs the individual Christian, it also robs the Church of fruitful ministry to individuals in a lost world and to the members of the body of Christ. *The Holy Spirit's purpose is to glorify Jesus Christ by communicating His presence and power here and now just as He did in the first century.* His power and presence are for you and for me! The person and purpose of the Holy Spirit are much too large and too mysterious to be fully described and defined in a book. Like all truth about God, these subjects are too immense for anyone to think that they have grasped them in their totality. We continue to learn as we grow in our knowledge of Him. We keep on learning how to stay in step with Him and be useful to Him.

In order to prepare this manuscript for publication, I added illustrations to the text from past occasions when the Holy Spirit manifested Himself in powerful and unusual ways to individual saints and groups of believers. I contacted these various men and women and asked them to tell their own stories. They responded enthusiastically to my requests to write their eyewitness accounts for this book. Our hearts rejoiced and were stirred afresh as we remembered those powerful times when heaven breathed upon us.

To all who have helped with this project I extend my deepest gratitude. Junko Blocksom tirelessly interpreted as I spoke in Japan. Paul R. Miller, an ICM missionary in Japan, kindly transcribed the messages from the tapes. Liz Willson volunteered to do some initial editing. Chris Momose, an ICM missionary in Kyoto, Japan, gave initial suggestions and encouragement. My daughter, Laura, with a degree in writing, and her husband, Dr. Randy Smith, who teaches creative writing in Belhaven College in Jackson, Mississippi, gave me challenging, stimulating, and encouraging suggestions regarding the arrangement and additional content the book should have. Della-Jane Brooks Healey, a new and dear friend—with her excellent writing skills—has given immense help with the readability, clarity, and flow of the material. Amy Shelor Clark, whom we have known since childhood, and who is a professional copy editor, assisted with the final preparation and form the book should have for publication. These two dear ladies were handpicked by God to assist me and are gifts of His kindness. Finally, my dear wife, Gerrie—what can I say? She has persevered with me by reading the manuscript chapter by chapter again and again and by helping me to see the changes I needed to make. She has demonstrated her usual patience, gentleness, and forbearance as I wrestled through certain issues necessary for the process.

I can ask for no greater blessing for each of you than for the Holy Spirit to refresh you with a deeper sense of the Lord Jesus' presence and power in your life than you have ever known.

For the reader of these pages, I pray that you will be deeply stirred to thirst for the reality and fullness of the Holy Spirit in your life and in your church. May heaven's richest blessing be upon you. This great blessing is none other than the revealed presence of Jesus Christ to you, in you, with you, and through you in streams of living water to both lost and saved—all for the glory of God.

Jerald (Jerry) R. White, Jr.
March 2005

Introduction

Lance is in his mid-twenties, a bright-faced, happy extrovert who bubbles with joy and love, a radiant Christian. Lance, as a non-Christian, met a young man from our church at work, who through several conversations introduced him to Jesus Christ as Lord and Savior. Lance had been a Christian a little more than two years when I began to meet with him each week. He thirsted to know God and His truth. In addition, he had a compelling desire to share with others what he knew about Jesus Christ, with both non-Christians and Christians. He witnessed wherever He went. He is now almost through seminary in his preparation for the ministry.

My purpose in meeting with Lance was to help establish him in the basics of the Christian life and to mentor him. I gave him reading assignments for particular books and asked him to study through Romans. He learned how to read the Bible attentively and carefully, how to let the Bible say what it says.

Each week Lance completed his study and then brought his notes to share with me what he had learned from God's Word. In one of our weekly meetings, we came to Romans 6:17: "But thanks be to God that though you were slaves of sin, you became obedient from the heart to that form of teaching to which you were committed." Lance then explained the meaning of the verse as he understood it. According to Lance, Paul was expressing thanks that even though these Roman Christians had been slaves to sin in their pagan condition, they were now obedient from the heart to the teaching that had been committed to them. I then asked Lance to read the verse again very carefully—word by word. He still did not see. I pointed out that Paul says, the "form of teaching to which you were committed." Because the Greek verb for the word *committed* is in the passive tense, the verse actually says, "You were committed *by* God *to* a form of teaching." Lance sat back in his chair; his face lit up with wonder and delight as he exclaimed, "Wow! That changes the whole meaning of the verse." I then shared with him that the Person of the Holy Spirit guided biblical writers in their choice of individual words—every word is important for an accurate understanding of the revealed truths. This verse in Romans actually teaches that God has committed us to a form of teaching. That form of teaching shapes us as we obey it from the heart—the believer's life is like plaster of paris being poured into the mold of Scripture. That is quite different from a form of teaching being given to us, or from our showing devotion to a type of teaching. Although both of these may be true, another point is being made here.

When we read, study, and meditate on the Bible, three questions should be in our thinking all the time. One cannot really understand the Word of God without asking these three questions:

1. What does it say? What do these words actually say? What do the nouns, verbs, adverbs, adjectives, prepositions, and other parts of speech say?
2. What does it mean? What is being communicated? What is the plain meaning of what is said rather than some secret, hidden meaning?
3. What does it mean for me? How does it apply to my life? What will I do with the promises, truths, and commands so that they are made real in my daily life?

A fourth question adds another important element to understanding God's Word: How does this portion of Scripture relate to the rest of the Bible? In other words, what does the rest of God's Word say about this particular truth? What is the context? Do other passages give further understanding for this passage? How does it compare with other similar passages of Scripture?

Some very sincere Christians bring their preconceived notions to the Bible and try to fit God's Word into their frame of thinking. This violates God's Word. We must let the Bible change our thinking rather than change the Bible to fit what we already think. God is the Original Communicator. He has communicated His truth clearly. He has given His children the Holy Spirit to be their indwelling Teacher. We diligently use our minds to think, study, and meditate on God's Word. The Holy Spirit assists in our understanding of God's Word by illumination and revelation. Illumination occurs when the Spirit enlightens our minds regarding God's truth. Revelation happens when He communicates His truth to our hearts.

Understanding this we can turn with listening and prepared hearts to what God has said about the reality and ministry of the Holy Spirit to every believer in every culture in every generation.

Gracious Father,

> *Please give us illumination as we go through this simple study. You have given us exceedingly great and precious promises that assure us of Your desire to fill us with Your Holy Spirit. We are most grateful that You want us to know and experience Your revealed presence. We now trust You to show us the way to enter into the wonderfully satisfying blessing You long to give us as Your children. With childlike faith we anticipate what You will do for Your own glory. Amen!*

CHAPTER ONE

Searching for Fullness

So I say to you, ask [keep asking],
and it will be given to you;
seek [keep seeking], and you will find;
knock [keep knocking],
and it will be opened to you.
—Luke 11:9 (includes marginal translations)

During the summer of 1965, the Lord poured out His Spirit in a dramatic way while I was speaking to a group of youth on retreat in Virginia. Wayne Barber—currently the senior teaching pastor at Hoffmantown Church in Albuquerque, New Mexico—was one of the youth ministers present at this meeting. He offers below his memories of this outpouring of the Holy Spirit upon this group of young people:

> I will never forget the first time in my life that I experienced firsthand God's mighty works in someone's life. I was in my early twenties and was working as a summer youth minister at Cave Spring Baptist Church in Cave Spring, Virginia. I took my youth group and joined with another friend of mine, and his

young people, for a few days of camp. We invited a young pastor named Jerry White to speak to us one particular night. Jerry arrived at the camp where we were staying probably an hour and a half before our program began. He wanted to pray with us before we went to the meeting, so we all three knelt beside the beds in one of the cabins. Jerry began to pray, and as he did he began to confess sin. I had never heard a man of God confess sin. In my mind at that time, I thought that men such as Jerry had arrived and that confession of sin was not a part of their lives. I will never forget the impression that God made on my mind in those glorious moments as this man honestly prayed before the Lord. The tears of remorse and the brokenness in his life were so real, and his heart was so tender towards God. Conviction was overwhelming in my life as he prayed, and though I didn't see it at the time, God was using this to help shape me for the rest of my own life.

After we spent what seemed to be only minutes, but turned out to be the better part of an hour, in prayer, we went down to the site where Jerry was to speak, an outdoor chapel with a creek running nearby. I was really worried about one young man in my group because he had a reputation for never paying attention and for disturbing our youth group talks and devotionals. This young man had found a frog and was already focusing his attention on it as the meeting began. We sang and then Jerry got up to preach. He directed us to Luke 5:1–11. As he spoke, the Spirit of God moved over our group. I have never witnessed anything like it. The young man about whom I was worried dropped the frog and could not take his eyes off our speaker. There was such a silence that it seemed almost loud. When Jerry gave the invitation, individuals responded so visibly that my friend and I didn't have a clue about what to do.

People fell to their knees in prayer. Some got up and moved away from the area where we had been seated. As I walked around, I saw people leading others to Christ; I saw one young person near the water kneeling and sobbing before the Lord. I saw adult chaperones kneeling and weeping before the Lord. These kinds of responses continued on and on and on. After Jerry left, my friend and I went to the cabin where we had prayed before the meeting. We asked God to continue moving on the group and to bring more of the young people to Christ. Periodically, our praying was interrupted by a knock at the cabin door. One of us would answer, and there would be a young person asking us to help him or her know the Savior personally. Over and over, one by one, they came to the cabin where we were.

This went on all through the night. It was the beginning of a journey that I am still on . . . Now, I am fifty-eight years old. God means more to me today than I ever could have dreamed at that camp thirty-seven years ago. But, the journey began that night for me. I had seen a vessel that God used! I had witnessed a man so filled with God's Spirit that God was free to use him. I had learned what John the Baptist so beautifully said—we must "decrease" so that "He might increase" . . . I will never be the same because of that glorious night.

It humbles and refreshes me to remember that afternoon, now almost forty years ago. I was surprised, blessed, and encouraged. It was a significant, confirming event for me at that time in my life. It was the first of many experiences I have been privileged to be a part of when the Holy Spirit came upon a group of people. Each time we knew it was a visitation from heaven, a manifestation of Jesus Christ here and now. I always long and pray for this, but the Sovereign God chooses when to give this gift of Self-disclosure, and to what degree. No man has control over these events.

My Search for Fullness

Let me tell you how I came to this place of longing and what led to these experiences. I had become a Christian at age sixteen between my junior and senior years in high school in Roanoke, Virginia. A few weeks after my conversion, I knew that it was God's will that I prepare for full-time ministry. I finished high school in 1956, met and married my wife (Gerald Hall, affectionately known as "little Gerrie") in 1959, and graduated from the University of Richmond with a degree in philosophy in 1960—but, for all these changes in my personal and professional life, I still knew so little about how to walk with God. No one ever discipled me or taught me the basics of Christian living. Therefore, I was spiritually ignorant and, as a result, powerless in my Christian life. My soul was full of sin and guilt and shame. I knew nothing about the ministry of the Holy Spirit that is so necessary for victory in the Christian life.

In the fall of 1960, I enrolled for my first year of seminary training at Southwestern Baptist Theological Seminary in Fort Worth, Texas. During this time, Gerrie and I attended a small, rural Baptist church just outside Fort Worth where Dr. Cal Guy, a missions professor at the seminary, was the pastor. During the summer break following my first year of seminary, Dr. Guy asked me to bring one of the Sunday evening messages because he had to be away. I was only twenty-three years old. When I began to prepare the message for that Sunday night worship service, my heart was dry, hard, and cold; my conscience convicted me. I only read my Bible for seminary classes, not for fellowship with God, and I did not even have a prayer life. Therefore, I had nothing to give in a message. Realizing my emptiness and my great need, I got up from the table where I was seated, went over by the sofa in the small apartment where we lived, and knelt down to pray. As I began to pray, the Lord Jesus, through the Holy Spirit, came to me and melted my heart. I saw with my heart what I had done against Him, and what in love He had done for me on the cross. I was broken in His presence. I repented with much weeping and was forgiven and cleansed in a fresh way. Some may think this was my true conversion, but there was no question that I had been truly converted at age sixteen. Even though I had been a Christian for seven years, I was still quite an infant in spiritual matters. This was like a new beginning for me. Needless to say, I had a message for Sunday night, which the Lord was pleased to use.

The long-term result of this new encounter was a compelling and perpetual hunger and thirst for spiritual reality. I knew there was more than what I had experienced in my first seven years as a Christian, and I wanted this deeper experience in my life. In addition, through exposure to biographies of respected and godly men like Charles G. Finney and Dwight L. Moody, I learned that the Holy Spirit *should* play as much of a role in the lives of Christians today as He did in the lives of first-century Christians about whom we read in the Bible. Thus began my search.

After two years of seminary training in Fort Worth, a friend, Dr. Charles G. Fuller, invited me to become his associate pastor at First Baptist Church in Roanoke, Virginia, a large downtown church. Dr. Fuller led the church to call me to this staff position with the understanding that I would finish my third year of seminary at Southeastern Baptist Theological Seminary in Wake Forest, North Carolina. I accepted, and moved with Gerrie and our two small children (Laura, age two, and Jeff, age three months) to Roanoke where I would serve the church on the weekends and attend seminary during the weekdays. All this time, my interest in and hunger for knowing the reality of the Holy Spirit in my life and ministry intensified.

The Southern Baptist denomination in which I served strongly emphasized evangelism and missions. However, during those years I do not remember much emphasis on discipleship for believers or on the ministry of the Holy Spirit. Most preaching focused on the cross of Jesus Christ and the love of God the Father, but there was little emphasis on the person and work of the Holy Spirit and on how we could know the reality of the Spirit in our daily lives. I was longing to know and understand how I could experience this reality.

I took a theological course on the doctrine of the Holy Spirit during my third and final year of seminary. The course surveyed the Holy Spirit's various works in the Old and New Testaments and examined the theological implications of these works. The material was historical and doctrinal, but the professor never discussed how the Holy Spirit could be appropriated and experienced today in our personal lives and corporately in our churches. I continued reading other books, searching for answers, and praying for this "something more" that I knew was real, but did not know how to have. Luke makes abundantly clear in the book of Acts that the coming of the Holy Spirit to fill first-century believers was the pivotal experience of the New Testament church. This was what gave early Christians power for life, witness, and ministry.

Based on my reading of the New Testament, I understood that I desperately needed this power. At the time, I was also troubled by the fact that what I saw in churches did not match what I read in the Bible. This was before I knew anything about any doctrinal (denominational) positions regarding the Holy Spirit's work. I only knew the Bible and the previously mentioned biographical accounts. My search continued.

One day I was looking over a book display at an evangelism conference for pastors. Standing beside me was a friend eight years older than I, a very large man who stood six foot seven and weighed 280 pounds. I picked up a book by R. A. Torrey, *The Baptism and Power of the Holy Spirit*. I looked up at this older and respected pastor and said, "I wonder about this. Can a man really know this?" He looked down at me and replied, "It's there if a man is willing to pay the price for it." That was not the answer I expected, nor the one for which I was looking. I wanted him to tell me what he knew about how I could know this reality in my own life and ministry. Did he know it in his life? Surely as a pastor he had wrestled with these questions and found the answer. Surely he could give me some guidance. But he did not, and my search continued.

Later, two well-known evangelists in my denomination came to First Baptist Church in Roanoke where I was still associate pastor. They came for a week of evangelistic services. One was a singer and the other a preacher. During the week, one of them wanted to walk to a Christian bookstore that was near our church. While walking back from the store, I turned to the evangelist with me and said, "I am very interested in this power of the Holy Spirit that I have read about. Do you ever wonder about the power of the Spirit in ministry?" The man never answered me. I thought surely he would know about the power of the Holy Spirit, how to live and minister in that power. But apparently, he did not. I kept on searching—thinking, praying, hungering, and reading.

Then one day while I was at the church office, Dr. Fuller stopped by my study. I began to tell him what I was thinking about and wrestling with in my mind, how close I felt to understanding something more about the Spirit's role in the believer's life. This dear friend and older mentor said to me, "Jerry, you are getting dangerously close." He understood from our conversation that I was drawing near to the reality and the truth that I was seeking. But I did not want to get close. I wanted to go the whole way into this reality that I knew was possible for every believer. I understood I needed something more of God's Spirit in my life and could not be content without it. I continued my search.

Because I was only working part-time in the church and going to seminary during the week, Gerrie and I did not have much money. Sometimes, I would go to the Christian bookstore, see a book that spoke to my hunger, and buy it. I would then have to go home and confess to Gerrie that I used some of our money to buy another book. Looking back, I now see that the Lord was leading me to certain books, which He used to teach me. As I read those books, bought with money we really could not afford to spend, little by little God taught me what I needed to know about the fullness of God's Spirit for life and ministry. I cannot emphasize strongly enough how ignorant I was about these truths.

A lady in our church gave me a biography of John Hyde (1865–1912) who was a Presbyterian missionary to India. In his biography is the following insightful account:

> "When I got on board the steamer at New York . . . bound for India for my life's work, I found in my cabin a letter addressed to me. It was in the handwriting of my father's friend. I opened and read it." It was not a long letter but the words leaped at John, burrowed into the depths of his soul, set there a flame of indignation upon the ashes of his pride. Said the minister friend, "I shall not cease praying for you, dear John, until you are filled with the Holy Spirit." The Holy

Spirit—that expression was to face John many times until at length he became fully filled and dynamically conscious of the Spirit.

"My pride was touched," John says of the incident, "and I felt exceedingly angry, crushed the letter, threw it into a corner of the cabin and went up on deck in a very angry spirit. The idea of implying that I was not filled with the Spirit!"

John was going as a missionary, he told himself, and it was presumptuous for him to go without being filled with the Holy Spirit; he was headed for the top, was he not? And as a natural condition, he thought himself Spirit-filled.

"And yet this man implied that I was not fitted and equipped for the work! I paced up and down that deck, a battle raging within. I felt very uncomfortable; I loved the writer, I knew the holy life he lived, and down in my heart was the conviction that he was right and that I was not fitted to be a missionary."

This was a battle not soon to be won, nor was John so constituted that he could turn from the fray with anything less than victory. He went back to his cabin, on his knees searched for the thrust-aside missive, and finding it, smoothed the paper out "and read it again and again. I still felt annoyed, but the conviction was gaining on me that my father's friend was right and I was wrong."

. . . The searching went on for a few days, during which John's soul was a tumult of misery . . .

"At last in despair, I asked the Lord to fill me with the Holy Spirit, and the moment I did this, the whole atmosphere was cleared up. I began to see myself and what selfish ambition I had. It was a struggle almost to the end of the voyage, but I was determined long before the port was reached, that whatever the cost, I would be really filled with the Spirit. The second climax came when I was led to tell the Lord I was willing even to fail in my language examinations in India, and be a missionary working quietly out of sight, that I would do anything and be anything, but the Holy Spirit I would have at any cost."[1]

The rest of John Hyde's story is the remarkable account of a man wholly filled with God's Spirit, and this alone explains his ministry.

When I finished reading this biography I wrote at the bottom of the last page, "The time and circumstances of the reading of this book were God appointed for my life. I shall never be the same, not because of this book, but because of the moments when God led me to read these pages. May God be praised for all His mercy! Lord, teach me how to pray! 12-15-64."

My Discovery of Fullness

In 1965, the summer after I finished seminary, my family and I went with my parents to Oklahoma, where my dad grew up and his family still lived. The six of us filled up my dad's car to make the two-day trip. I took two new books that I had purchased to read along the way—*Abide in Christ* by Andrew Murray and *Simple Things of the Christian Life* by G. Campbell Morgan. As a twenty-six-year-old man, I was still searching for what I needed to know so that the Holy Spirit could be more to me than just someone I read about in the Bible who worked powerfully in the lives of first-century Christians, or men like "Praying Hyde," as John Hyde became affectionately known. On that long journey to Oklahoma, we took turns driving. While my dad drove, I sat with my wife and our two small children in the cramped back seat and read *Abide in Christ*. It was nourishing my soul and instructing me in a quality of Christian life about which I knew little. As I read, Gerrie, who was sitting beside me, began reading over my shoulder. She turned to me with tears in her eyes (Gerrie does not show tears very often) and said, "I have never read anything like this in my life." Our souls were being fed with the truth about how Jesus can be real in your life. As we traveled,

I would read one book for a while, put it down, and then read the other one. There was a lot to think about.

During our visit in Oklahoma, our whole family was at my grandmother's house. One afternoon, because my compelling hunger to know the truth about the Spirit continued to grow within me, I left my grandmother's house and went down the street to my great aunt's house to be alone with the Lord. I felt I needed to pray and to read. At this time I was reading my other book, *Simple Things of the Christian Life*, by G. Campbell Morgan. Dr. Morgan was an outstanding teacher of God's Word in England in the first half of the nineteen hundreds. This paperback book had cost me ninety-five cents, which was a lot to us in those lean times. I have kept that book these thirty-seven years because of its significance in my younger life. That summer day in 1965 I read these words:

> Holiness does not depend upon your effort at all. Holiness simply depends upon your abandoning yourself to the indwelling Spirit of God, that He may maintain in health the life which He has Himself communicated. The power for holiness is not in the flesh, but in the Spirit. The way in which man can live the Christ-life in health and strength, and ever-increasing strength, is simply that of answering the call of the life within him. It is true there are responsibilities. What are they? Briefly stated they include— first, a renunciation of all things of which the life of God disapproves; second, an abandonment of the whole being to God, that He may possess the territory, and realize it according to His will, and for His glory; third, the maintaining of simple quiet trust in Him, which expresses itself in obedience and patient waiting for His guidance.[2]

All of a sudden I understood! God had enabled me to know what He desired of me. The truth for which I had been searching for four years was finally revealed to my heart. It was now clear what I needed to do to cooperate with God so I could enter into the fullness He wanted me to have. I got up from the sofa where I was seated and got down on my face, prostrate on the floor. There I did what I had read in Dr. Morgan's book. I confessed all my sins. I abandoned my life to God for anything He wanted. I told Him I would—in simple faith— trust Him for His fullness. He had commanded this in Ephesians 5:18 when He said, "Do not get drunk with wine, for that is dissipation, but *be filled with the Spirit*" (italics added). The Holy Spirit filled all the believers at Pentecost (Acts 2) and at other times recorded in Acts. If fullness was for all believers in the New Testament church, and was commanded by God in Ephesians 5, then it must be for me too. I could quietly trust Him to keep His Word, yield completely to His Lordship, and be filled with the Holy Spirit.

Because of dramatic encounters with the Holy Spirit that I had read about other men experiencing, I thought, prior to this, that I needed a similar experience. These kinds of encounters certainly happened in the book of Acts. So, for a period of time, I sought an experience with God like I had read about. But I finally came to understand that God gives experiences when, and to whom, He chooses. The issue was not to have some great and thrilling experience, but rather, to trust God to keep His Word, even if I felt nothing. The important point was to have a relationship with God of cleanliness, abandonment, and trust.

That July day I felt no emotion; it was not an extraordinary experience. I quietly entered into an agreement with God that I was totally His for whatever He wanted, and I would trust Him to keep His Word. You see, He had promised in Luke 11:13, "If you then, being evil, know how to give good gifts to your children, how much more shall your heavenly Father give the Holy Spirit to those who ask Him?" As a father of a small daughter and son, I understood that. So I chose to trust Him for this great provision for my great need. I was determined to hold on to His promise.

I got up from the floor where I had been lying face down, in submission and worship, and wrote at the bottom of the page in the book I was reading, "7-25-65." I inscribed the date to remember that on this day I had entered by simple faith and submission into a relationship of total surrender and trust with God. This meant I would endeavor to live cleanly before Him and to do whatever He wanted of me.

My Failures and God's Faithfulness

My understanding of what it meant to be Spirit-filled and to live a victorious life was not biblically accurate. In my immaturity and ignorance, I thought I would live above my circumstances, hardly touched by the things which before had plagued me or caused me to stumble. Life would be radically different now. I knew very little about the world, the flesh, and the devil. God was now going to introduce me to more truth about walking in the Spirit. I would soon be tested.

On our return trip from Oklahoma to Virginia, I got upset with my dad about something. I don't even remember what it was. This was my first lesson that the Spirit's fullness does not suddenly take away immaturity. The devil taunted me, "You are no different. Nothing has happened to you. If you are abandoned to God and Spirit-filled, how can you behave as you have?" I knew I could not ignore my wrong attitude and actions; I could not pretend that these things did not happen. Because of the commitment I had made just a few days earlier and the command to maintain a clear conscience before God, I knew I must apologize to my dad and ask him to forgive me. It was not easy, but I had committed to God to do anything He wanted of me. He desired that I should repent to Him and to my father. So I did. I died to my pride, chose against my flesh, and asked both God and my dad to forgive me. It was very humbling. I held on to God's Word that He would fill me for the asking (Luke 11:13).

A few days after returning home, I was scheduled to speak one afternoon at a youth retreat in Virginia (the same camp retreat that Wayne Barber talks about in the opening testimonial of this chapter). Several churches had joined together to have this retreat for about sixty-five youth. Two young men who were friends of mine were serving as summer youth directors for two of the churches. Before the afternoon meeting, I asked the two youth pastors, Wayne and Andy, to pray with me for the meeting. We went into a little room where they slept. We knelt down by one of the bunk beds on the bare wood floor. Wayne knelt on one side of me, and Andy on the other side. I began to pray. While we were kneeling there before the Lord, the Holy Spirit convicted me very specifically. It was as though He said, "There is sin in your heart. Confess it." I thought to myself, "Confess my sin in front of these guys?" The answer within was quite clear, "Yes!" I thought, "What will they think? They will never respect me again." The Holy Spirit reminded me that in Oklahoma I had gotten down on my face and prayed, "Anything God, no matter what." So again, I died to my pride and began to confess my sins out loud in prayer. I would confess a sin, and another would come to mind. Then I would confess it, then another. There was lust in my heart, pride, and even coldness of heart. I thought I had taken God at His word to be filled with the Spirit. How could all this ugliness be there if I was filled with the Spirit? I called on God for mercy to forgive me. I trusted Him again for fullness and asked that He would do a work at this retreat. We got up from praying, and those men did not say one word to me. Of course, I sure wondered what they were thinking, because even I had never heard anyone confess his sin out loud before others.

We went down the long winding stairs that led to a little cement dock beside the creek that ran through the forest camp. The high-school youth and their adult counselors sat on one end of the dock and on the rocky bank beside the dock. I stood on the other end of the dock. With the sound of the gurgling creek behind me, I spoke on Luke 5:1–11 about Peter and his partners fishing all night in the Sea of Galilee and catching nothing. They were washing their nets on the shore of the lake when Jesus directed them to launch out into the deep to fish again. Peter told Jesus that they had fished all night and had caught nothing, but at Jesus' word they would try again. When they did, they filled the nets to the point of breaking with a great catch of fish, enough to fill up their boat and their fishing partners' boat. Both boats became so full that they began to sink. Peter was greatly humbled by this amazing miracle he knew Jesus had done, and as a result, he saw his own sinfulness. The point I made in this message was very simple: We can do our very best to live the Christian life in fleshly effort, but we will fail. When we yield our all to Jesus, and in simple trust and obedience do whatever He says, He gives victory. I then dismissed the youth and chaperones to go out and pray by themselves for several minutes. Wayne came over to me, put his head on my shoulder, and cried. He said, "I've never experienced anything like this before in my life!" Shortly afterwards, I had to leave to drive back home, only to learn later that the Holy Spirit fell on those young people and their counselors. They dismissed the rest of the program for the afternoon, and the majority of those sixty-five youth made decisions for Christ, with several committing themselves to full-time ministry.

Through this experience, God said to me, "It is real. I have kept My Word." That was the beginning. I was very encouraged, but still hungry to know more, and was very aware of how little I yet understood.

My Wife's Search for Fullness

God continued changing attitudes and behaviors in my life, and Gerrie witnessed it. Seeing these changes take place in me made her aware of her own need. She began to wonder how she could know the fullness of God's Spirit in her life. Please understand, I am not talking about having some dramatic experience, although that sometimes happens. I am talking about a relationship whereby God's Spirit can have your whole being to do with you and through you whatever He wants. It is a relationship with the Holy Spirit, a relationship of a fully yielded, cleansed, and trusting life depending on Him.

In 1967, while I was pastor of Central Baptist Church in Altavista, Virginia, a book arrived in the mail one day from a friend. It was a classic book greatly used by Baptist missionaries in China in the late 1920s and '30s to introduce people to the Spirit-filled life. This small, brief but powerful book by L. L. Legters was appropriately titled *The Simplicity of the Spirit-Filled Life*. Even though the book was sent to me, Gerrie remains quite sure that it was sent for her! The Lord had already prepared Gerrie's heart, and she was ripe to learn about how she could have the fullness of God's Spirit in her life. She took the book, read it, and very quickly learned what had taken me several years to learn.

Shortly thereafter, while at home by herself, she was spending time alone with the Lord. Our children were in school. After reading her Bible, she went and knelt down on the green rug by a chair in our living room. Making this her altar before the Lord, she entered into a wonderful relationship with the Lord that allowed God to fill her with Himself in the Person of the Holy Spirit. It was a quiet act of complete surrender and faith, just as mine had been. When she got up and resumed her Bible reading, she could immediately tell that something had changed within her. (She will tell about this experience in her own words later in this book.)

Some time later, Gerrie was correcting our children in the hallway that led to our bedrooms. Our daughter Laura, who was ten years old, looked up at her mother and said, "Mama, something has happened to you. You're different. You don't yell at us like you used to." This was confirmation to Gerrie that God had kept His promise. She quickly realized the difference the fullness of God's Spirit had made in her life.

My Daughter's Desire for Fullness

In 1971, we were still serving at Central Baptist Church. We were having a worship service with a missionary as our guest speaker that Sunday. At the close of the service, I was standing at the front during a time of invitation for people to make decisions regarding their relationship with Christ. I felt someone tug at my coat, and when I looked down, I saw our Laura. I bent over, and she whispered in my ear, "Daddy, I want to be filled with the Holy Spirit." I thought she probably did not understand the real meaning of her request and that I would need to explain this further to her. She was just a child. How could she understand filling by the Spirit? Was this just some childish whim? I told her that I would talk with her about it later at home. Because we were in a series of special church meetings, two or three days passed before I spoke with her. Finally, I suggested that we go to her room, and I would talk with her about becoming Spirit-filled. She replied, "I already am." I asked her to tell me about it, which she did. She understood exactly what her mother and I had come to understand. She knew what to do. She had gone to her room and worked it out with the Lord. She entered into that relationship with the Lord known as the Spirit-filled life, even as a child. Jeff, our son, was younger and did not understand yet. What a difference the Spirit's fullness made in her life. No longer did she fuss or argue with her little brother. Instead, she expressed love for him and concern for his spiritual need. Peace ruled in their relationship.

In the years that followed, I had the privilege of sharing with others what I had learned. I taught these truths in many traditional Baptist churches. I spoke of the Spirit at retreats and conferences. I prayed with missionaries and pastors who desired to know the reality of the Spirit in their lives and ministries and wanted to enter the Spirit's fullness. Even though they had faithfully served the Lord in ministry, they had not known the reality of the Spirit-filled life.

My Parents Discover Fullness

During the 1970s, my own mother and dad attended retreats at The Master's Inn, a retreat center I had founded in central Virginia. The center was located in a lovely setting—a large three-story log house on forty acres of wooded land with gently rolling hills. We conducted various kinds of weekend retreats for fifteen to twenty-four people. Mom and Dad attended most of the retreats with a hunger for God's Word. I watched as the Lord did a significant work in their lives through the truths they learned. My mother, Una White, tells below about her entrance into the Spirit-filled life:

> I was reared in a Christian home, but not until I was seventeen and away at business college did I invite Jesus into my heart and life.
>
> I attended Sunday school and church, but discovered later that biblical teaching was somewhat lacking, and my spiritual growth was also lacking. I experienced "dry" periods in my life, and from time to time, I attended church irregularly. Eventually, my husband and I became more involved with church life by faithful attendance and serving in various ways.
>
> However, we were not taught about the filling of the Holy Spirit. I knew that the Lord commands us to be filled with the Spirit, as we see in Ephesians 5 and in other Scriptures. But, I interpreted these passages

to mean that we were to invite Jesus into our hearts and receive His Spirit.

My husband and I were blessed to attend retreats conducted and taught by our son at The Master's Inn in Altavista, Virginia. Here we learned the real meaning of the filling of the Holy Spirit. During one of those retreats, I prayed and asked God to fill me with His Spirit. It was a gentle and joyful experience; I was aware of His presence as never before. He took control and relieved me of fear and anxiety. I had peace in my innermost being beyond description. He gave me a deeper hunger for the Word. He empowered me to serve and minister to young adults in Sunday school. He prepared me to share Christ with those outside the church, and He gave me a love for missions.

Through the storms and deep sorrows of life, He is my refuge and my strength. I ask God daily to fill me continually with the Holy Spirit. I praise His Holy Name!

My Search for More Understanding

The discovery of God's fullness on that summer day in 1965 was the most life-changing truth since my conversion ten years earlier.

As I have grown spiritually, there have been other life-changing truths learned: the glorious basic truths found in the book of Romans; the reality of spiritual warfare with a very real enemy; and the primacy of fellowship with God sought through private worship, Bible meditation, and prayer.

Learning the truths of God, and ever learning them deeper, is the way for every disciple. I have continued my search through prayer and meditation on the Word of God. I have read many books on the subject of the Holy Spirit, some scholarly writings and others, devotional or pastoral in approach. I have also read many books on true, heaven-sent revival, which involves the Holy Spirit manifesting God's presence to a group of people, as we see in Acts. I am persuaded that this, the power of the Holy Spirit, is what is definitely and sadly lacking in most of Christendom.

There are different positions taken by godly men on the work and ministry of the Holy Spirit. All positions are by sincere Christians attempting to explain the Person and purpose of the Holy Spirit. There has been a great debate in Christendom over just how the Holy Spirit works, and what to expect when He does. There is the Charismatic position, the Pentecostal position, and the evangelical position. I do not want to present to you a particular position, but rather, I will let God's Word speak. Like all truth about God, you cannot put this infinite truth about the Person and work of the Holy Spirit into a neat little package, as if the whole subject could be covered and understood. The Holy Spirit is an infinite Person who is infinitely creative. In no way have I learned all the truth about the Holy Spirit—this infinite truth cannot be comprehended fully with a finite mind. There are basics, however, that any believer can and should know. To attempt to confine the doctrine about Him in a system of truth is foolish. We can never fully understand Him. We can never fully outline His work. We can never explain all about Him. There will always be a mystery about Him. It is part of "the mystery of godliness" (1 Timothy 3:16). But we can and should rejoice and enjoy Him and His fullness ministering in our lives.

Faithful and loving Father,

You promised that if we would keep asking we would receive. Because of Your infinite love, You want to give even more than we want to ask. Thank You that as we seek, You keep leading us to what we need to know so that we can experience more of Your fullness and presence. Nothing satisfies the depth of our souls like You. Please reveal Your truth to our hearts. Amen!

Notes

[1] Basil Miller, *Praying Hyde*, (Grand Rapids, Michigan: Zondervan Publishing House, 1964), 16–18.

[2] G. Campbell Morgan, *Simple Things of the Christian Life*, (Westwood, New Jersey: Fleming H. Revell Company, 1963), 36.

CHAPTER TWO

Another Helper Like Jesus

I will ask the Father, and He will give you another
Helper [Comforter, Advocate, Intercessor],
that He may be with you forever.
—John 14:16 (includes marginal translation)

Many decades have passed since I first prostrated myself on that rug, calling on God to fill me with His Spirit. I have prayed that prayer countless times. I am aware of my need for His fullness far more now than I was then. I have continued to seek, and God has continued to teach me. My journey, perhaps like yours, has been one of continual seeking and finding, continual thirsting and drinking.

On January 12, 2002, my Dad closed his eyes to this world and stepped into heaven. After eighty-five years of superb health, he unexplainably began to lose weight in his eighty-sixth year. The doctors could not find the cause. By the time they found the cancerous tumor in the top part of his stomach, the disease had entered the lymph nodes around his stomach, and within five months he was gone from us.

As an only child, I strongly felt a responsibility for my parents. They had been married almost sixty-four years and loved each other dearly. They were an excellent example of love and devotion in marriage. Being a close, loving family—but living nine hundred miles from them—made it difficult to care for them. Several trips and many phone calls were needed as we journeyed through those sorrowful days.

Dad was a very talented musician who, as a young man, entered the field of education as a high-school band director. He served in the army during World War II. He resumed his band director position upon returning from the war and later moved into school administration as assistant principal in the same school, and then as principal. He completed his career in his early sixties as the assistant superintendent in another school system and retired. In retirement he continued to be very active in leadership roles, both in his church, and outside with the organization for retired teachers of Virginia.

His hobby was woodworking, which began when he took woodworking classes in high school in a small Oklahoma town. As in all things he did, his craftsmanship was excellent.

Dad was a wonderful father. He loved me. He prayed for me. He encouraged me. He was always excited about my ministry. He gave me gifts to express his love. He was a leader among men, both outside the church and inside the church. He was greatly respected by his large church family and its pastors. His funeral was a wonderful tribute to him, as well as a glorious time of worship and praise to God.

I knew that one day my parents would go to be with the Lord. After his illness was diagnosed, I tried to prepare mentally for my dad's departure. As a pastor for forty years, I have been through this many times with others. I had been through it with our daughter Laura when she lost her younger son, Jonathan, to cancer at the age of five, another very sorrowful chapter in our family's biography! Even though I tried to get ready for my dad's departure, I was not prepared for the emotional earthquake it was to my soul. For sixty-three years of my life, he was always there, always loving, always ready to give counsel when I needed it, always smiling when I would see him, always praying for me. Suddenly, even though his home going was anticipated, the words reverberated in my soul like a loud voice shouting in a large, empty room, "DAD IS GONE!" Now I would only see his smiling face in pictures. I would never be able to sit and talk with him again. I would never feel his loving hug again. I would never feel his arm around me again as he prayed for me. I would never receive that punctual 7:00 PM Saturday phone call from him again. Dad was gone, never to return. The emotional vacancy his absence left was far more than I expected. Even with a very loving and devoted wife, a married daughter and son, six grandchildren on earth, and a loving and praying mom, no one could take the unique place that a loving dad holds.

Sitting beside my chair in my study is a beautiful walnut wood floor lamp that my dad made when he was sixteen years old. Every morning when I go to have a time with the Lord, I touch it to turn it on, but it is not him. It is just something he made. I have an excellent portrait that was made of him for his eightieth birthday, but it is not Dad. Last Sunday I wore one of his favorite ties, but it is not Dad. All I truly have is the memory of him. One day I picked up a micro-cassette recorder that I found among his possessions when we cleaned out his things. I pushed the play button, and there was his voice telling some of his life story for his grandchildren and their families. I listened for a moment and was overcome with the sense of loss, the utter vacancy. Tears flowed. Gushing up from the depths of my being was fresh grief. The important place he occupied at the head of our family was empty. "DAD IS GONE!" You may have felt the same loss of a dear loved one and occasionally have moments of renewed pain and an overwhelming sense of loss.

When loved ones are gone, all we have left are memories, or pictures, or things that belonged to them. Relics! But we no longer have *them*. They are gone forever. I remember our daughter Laura saying months after her Jonathan died, "I would give anything if I could just hold him for five minutes, feel his soft hair against my face and touch his skin." That precious, vibrant, round-faced, blond-headed boy was gone, never to return. Yet, in her words, her arms "ached to hold him again."

A profound and wonderful contrast exists between the departure of a loved one and Jesus. With Jesus, we do not hold mere memories and treasures and relics He left behind, but we have Him. In the Person of the Holy Spirit, we have Jesus—alive and real and with us always. The disciples' experience with the death of a loved one or friend was the same as ours. Death meant final departure. The disciples were beginning to understand Jesus' plain words that soon

He would be crucified. Their souls must have been shaken that He was about to die. Their beloved Master and Lord, for whom they had forsaken all, was going to depart from them.

Already they felt the impending loss of their beloved Lord and Friend just as we feel the loss of a dear loved one. The idea of His resurrection was hard for them to grasp. It had never happened before in all of human history. John records Jesus' words, "But now I am going to Him who sent Me; and none of you asks Me, 'Where are You going?' But because I have said these things to you, sorrow has filled your heart" (John 16:5–6). Luke speaks of their emotional state in his account of Gethsemane, "And when He rose from prayer, He came to the disciples and found them sleeping from sorrow" (Luke 22:45).

Imagine what it must have been like for these disciples. What would they do if Jesus left them? They had left all to follow Him for three years. Being with Him brought them a profound sense of security and peace. He loved them like no one else ever had. He took care of them. He answered all their questions. He revealed God clearly to them. He never confronted a situation that defeated Him. Whatever He faced, He was always more than sufficient, always triumphant. When Legion came running to Him indwelt with five or six thousand demons, Jesus set him free (Mark 5:1–13). Standing in front of a tomb where a friend was buried who had been dead four days, Jesus called Lazarus to come out to live again (John 11:1–46). When five thousand people were hungry, He took five loaves of bread and two fishes and fed them all (Mark 6:30–46). When a storm on the lake threatened to swamp their boat and drown them, Jesus stood and by a mere word calmed the storm (Mark 4:35–41). By these things and so much more they knew this was the Son of God. Immanuel! God Himself with us! Was there now any hope if He left? What would happen to their lives? What would happen regarding the Kingdom of God He spoke about? They were filled with fearful helplessness. Their future was shrouded in the darkness of uncertainty.

The Holy Spirit in the Old Testament

Before we look at what Jesus promised regarding the coming of the Holy Spirit, let's do a brief overview about what the disciples understood about the Holy Spirit from their Scriptures. In the Old Testament, the Spirit of God appears first in Genesis 1:2, "And the Spirit of God was moving [*hovering*, marginal translation] over the surface of the waters." In Exodus 31:3, 31 we learn that Bezalel was filled with the Spirit of God to equip him for the construction of the tabernacle. Joshua was a man in whom was the Spirit of God for leadership of the Israelites (Numbers 27:18). The book of Judges speaks of the Spirit of God being upon the judges for their task as leaders (Judges 3:10; 6:34; 11:29; 13:25; 14:6, 19; and 15:14). After King David's sin with Bathsheba, followed by his deep repentance, he prayed in Psalm 51:11, "Do not cast me away from Your presence / And do not take Your Holy Spirit from me." He did not want to lose God's anointing for leading the people as their king. Ezekiel testifies in 11:5, "Then the Spirit of the Lord fell upon me." Isaiah 11:2–3 and 42:1 foretells that the Messiah will have the Spirit of God upon Him. Joel 2:28–29 prophesies that God will pour out His Spirit on all flesh, not meaning pagans and Christians alike, but rather all those who are the Lord's, not just certain ones like prophets and kings. Many other Scriptures in the Old Testament speak of the Holy Spirit, but this sampling gives us an overview.

What do we consistently see through these and other Scriptures? The Holy Spirit. He is God's power enabling ordinary believers to perform God's will. Whatever the task, the Holy Spirit is God's power in action through men and women. What He bids them to do He empowers them to do.

The Holy Spirit in Jesus' Life

Jesus was fully human, but without sin and without a sin nature like ours (Romans 8:3). His life on earth as God's only and perfect Son cannot be explained apart from the Holy Spirit. The Spirit was absolutely necessary for everything regarding Jesus' life. Nothing about Him makes sense without the Spirit.

The Spirit caused Mary to conceive God's Son. She became pregnant with Jesus by the Spirit's miraculous work. This does not mean she had a relationship with the Holy Spirit like a man with a woman. Pagan religions of that day believed that the gods could have sexual relationships with women. The Bible is very clear in its wording. When Mary questioned how she could be the mother of God's Son when she was a virgin, the Bible records the answer, "The angel answered and said to her, 'The Holy Spirit will come upon you, and the power of the Most High will overshadow you; and for that reason the holy Child shall be called the Son of God'" (Luke 1:35).

The Holy Spirit came upon Jesus at His baptism by John the Baptist, which was Jesus' inauguration into public ministry from His private life as a carpenter (Matthew 3:13–17). The Spirit who filled Him then led Jesus into a barren wilderness to be tempted by the devil, which was a testing by His Father (Luke 4:1–13). When Jesus came out of the wilderness after the temptation, the Bible says, "And Jesus returned to Galilee in the *power* of the Spirit" (v. 14, italics added). His victory over the devil in severe temptation and testing must have prepared Him to return in the power of the Spirit for His ministry to lost, hurting humanity.

The Holy Spirit empowered Jesus to perform miracles. Quite significantly Luke 5:17 says, "One day He was teaching; and there were some Pharisees and teachers of the law sitting there, who had come from every village of Galilee and Judea and from Jerusalem; and the power of the Lord was present for Him to perform healing." If Jesus always had the power to heal any time and any place, then why would the Bible point out this fact here? Without the Holy Spirit's power Jesus could not have performed miracles. Acts 2:22 also points out the same truth. "Men of Israel, listen to these words: Jesus the Nazarene, a man attested to you by God with miracles and wonders and signs which God performed through Him in your midst." By what means would God do these miracles through Jesus? By the same means He had always worked His wonders. The Spirit is God's power in action, and this is how God worked miracles through Jesus.

The Holy Spirit was the power necessary for Jesus' resurrection from the grave and His enthronement in heaven (Ephesians 1:19–21). Without the almighty power of the Holy Spirit Jesus could not have been raised from the dead with a new resurrected body, nor could He have passed through the heavens to His everlasting place on the throne of heaven. The Holy Spirit was also the means by which He gave instructions to His disciples after His resurrection. Acts 1:2 reports, "After He had *by the Holy Spirit* given orders to the apostles whom He had chosen" (italics added). Even His speaking to the apostles in a resurrection appearance was through the Holy Spirit.

Jesus' entire life from His conception through His life, ministry, death, resurrection, ascension, enthronement, and final orders to His apostles was by the means of the Holy Spirit. The Spirit empowered the very human Jesus to accomplish the will of God. Nothing about Him can be explained apart from the Spirit.

Gerald F. Hawthorne wrote that the gospel writers agree on two fundamental matters: First, Jesus was indeed a human being, a genuine human person, having all the limitations that pertain to humanity. Second, he says that the significance of the Spirit in Jesus' life is this: "that the Holy Spirit was the divine power by which Jesus overcame his human limitations, rose above his human weakness, and won out over his human mortality."[1]

The Spirit Promised

When Jesus was preparing to depart from the earth, He promised that His followers would have the same Holy Spirit that He experienced in His life. Luke 24:49 records His words to His disciples, "And behold, I am sending forth the promise of my Father upon you; but you are to stay in the city until you are clothed with power from on high." They were witnesses to Jesus' death as God's substitute for the sins of mankind and His resurrection to defeat death. Jesus had given them the message of repentance for forgiveness of sins that they were to proclaim throughout the world (Luke 24:44–48). But He told them to wait until He clothed them with heaven's power. John the Baptist foretold, "As for me, I baptize you with water for repentance, but He who is coming after me is mightier than I, and I am not fit to remove His sandals; He will baptize you with the Holy Spirit and fire" (Matthew 3:11). Heaven's work on earth can only be done with heaven's power. The disciples' future ministry had to have the power of the Holy Spirit or they were doomed to failure.

Jesus' command to wait for the promise of power from on high stood on the foundation of His teaching in John 14–16, which contains His most complete instruction regarding the Holy Spirit. He had already comforted them in John 14:1 by saying, "Do not let your heart be troubled; believe in God, believe also in Me." In John 14:16, Jesus spoke further comfort to His disciples about what He was going to do for them after His departure. "I will ask the Father, and He will give you another Helper, that He may be with you forever." This must have brought additional comfort to their sorrowful souls. He then punctuated His promise of a Helper with an extraordinary follow-up promise, "I will not leave you as orphans; I will come to you" (v.18). The Helper He promised to come is none other than the Spirit of Christ Himself.

When Jesus promised "another" Helper, He used a particular Greek word. Two Greek words can be translated "another." One word means "another of a different kind." My wife is "another" person, which means that as a female she is different from me. The other word means "another of the same kind." My son, as a male, is "another" person of the same kind. Jesus used the word for "another of the same kind." Jesus promised that He was going to send another Person like Himself. The Spirit is not an "it" or an impersonal power. He is "another Helper" exactly like Jesus. All that Jesus is, He is.

Greek scholars tell us that there is not one English word that adequately translates the Greek word we find in our Bible as "Helper" or "Counselor." Those are the nearest words, but they do not communicate the full meaning of the Greek word. (I understand it is the same in Japanese.) The Greek word literally means, "one called alongside to help." Other words that convey some of the meaning are Comforter, Advocate, Encourager, Intercessor, Strengthener, and Stand-by. One scholar suggested that the Greek word is best understood as "legal friend."

I have a very good friend who is a judge. Before becoming a judge he was my lawyer. Suppose that during the time my friend was my lawyer, someone decided to sue me. If I went to another lawyer who did not know me, I would become his client, and he would defend me because I would pay him for his services. If, however, I went to my dear friend, Doug, to serve as my lawyer, not only would he do a good job because I would pay him for his services, but because he loves me he would do his very best for me. He would be my legal friend, and out of his love for me he would counsel me, defend me, pray for me, and be my helper. The major difference between my friend and the Holy Spirit is this: My good friend is a mere man; the Holy Spirit is God the Spirit. My friend would be confined to his area of expertise. The Holy Spirit is qualified for every area of my life. My friend would be a person I would have to go see. The Spirit would ever be present with me because He lives in me. This Person is the Spirit of Christ who comes to dwell in you at conversion. Jesus said, "That He may be with you *forever*" (John 14:16, italics added). He further said, "He abides *with* you and will be *in* you" (John 14:17, italics added). The beloved Savior would be taken to heaven; His beloved Spirit would be sent to His disciples and to every believer. In this way Jesus is more to His followers by His Spirit than He could ever be if He was still present in His flesh. By His Spirit Jesus can be with and in every believer, every moment, being all each one needs, rather than being confined to one place because of the limitation of a human body. He will help you in your every need. He will counsel you in every decision. He will comfort you in distress and pain. He will encourage you when there is much to discourage you. He will stand by you in your failures. He will help you to pray. He will pray for you, especially when you know not what to pray. He will be your most personal, intimate, and trusted Friend. This Helper will be all that Jesus is—personally for you—never, no never, to leave you or fail you.

The Spirit's Purpose

Jesus spoke further about this Helper in John 14:17 as the Spirit of truth. He is our resident Teacher to teach us what God says in His Word and how it applies personally to our lives. The Spirit uses God-called teachers to help us understand God's Word, but He alone can open our minds to understand the Scriptures with our hearts. He alone can reveal, illumine, and apply God's Word and cause it to be alive, real, and personal so that we are nourished, energized, and refreshed. He alone can show us how to live the truth, and give us strength to do so.

The Holy Spirit's assignments are many but with one purpose. He came to glorify Jesus Christ (John 15:26, 16:14). His many ministries are for the purpose of revealing, magnifying, and honoring Christ. A few of those ministries are: He convicts non-believers of sin (John 16:8); He illumines and gives revelation (John 16:14); He causes new birth (John 3:8); He immerses believers into the Body of Christ (1 Corinthians 12:13); He seals the converted (Ephesians 1:13); He indwells each of God's children (Romans 8:9); He witnesses to believers' hearts, giving assurance they are God's children (Romans 8:16); He transforms them into the likeness of Jesus (2 Corinthians 3:18); He equips saints for ministry by giving spiritual gifts (1 Corinthians 12:7); He fills the hungry and thirsty with God's fullness (John 7:37–39); and He empowers believers for living a holy life and ministering the life and love of Jesus to others (Romans 8:3–4, 12–14; Ephesians 1:18–23; 1 Corinthians 12–14).

In his book, *Keep in Step with the Spirit*, Dr. J. I. Packer explains the Spirit's purpose quite clearly using a wonderful illustration. He wrote:

> The essence of the Holy Spirit's ministry, at this or any time in the Christian era, is to mediate the presence of our Lord Jesus Christ . . . The Holy Spirit's distinctive new covenant role, then, is to fulfill what we may call a floodlight ministry in relation to the Lord Jesus Christ . . . I remember walking to a church one winter evening to preach on the words 'he shall glorify me,' seeing the building floodlit as I turned the corner, and realizing that this was exactly the illustration my message needed. When floodlighting is well done, the floodlights are so placed that you do not see them; you are not in fact supposed to see where the light is coming from; what you are meant to see is just the building on which the floodlights are trained. The intended effect is to make it visible when otherwise it would not be seen for the dark-

ness, and to maximize its dignity by throwing all its details in to relief so that you see it properly. This perfectly illustrates the Spirit's new covenant role. He is, so to speak, the hidden floodlight shining on the Saviour.

Or think of it this way. It is as if the Spirit stands behind us, throwing light over our shoulder, on Jesus, who stands facing us. The Spirit's message to us is never, 'Look at me; listen to me; come to me; get to know me,' but always, 'Look at *him*, and see his glory; listen to *him*, and hear his word; go to *him*, and have life; get to know *him*, and taste his gift of joy and peace.' (Packer's italics)[2]

Jesus said, "When the Helper comes, whom I will send to you from the Father, that is the Spirit of truth who proceeds from the Father, He will testify about Me" (John 15:26).

A Relationship of Love

The heart and soul of a relationship with God the Father and Jesus Christ the Lord is love. This is not ordinary human love; rather it is a love beyond human emotion and affection. It is a quality of love that is self-sacrificing for the highest good of another without any expectations of a return benefit. It is love where God alone is its source. John 13:1 contains a tender reference to this kind of love Jesus had for His disciples. "Now before the Feast of the Passover, Jesus knowing that His hour had come that He would depart out of this world to the Father, having loved His own who were in the world, He loved them to the end" (margin, "to the uttermost; or eternally"). He then commanded them to love each other with the same kind of love with which He loved them (John 13:34). Then He said, "If you love Me, you will keep My commandments" (John 14:15).

The obvious inference is that this quality of love Jesus has for His followers is the kind of love that will motivate them to obey Him. He further expounds this essential truth when He says, "If anyone loves Me, he will keep My word; and My Father will love him, and We will come to him and make Our abode with him" (John 14:23). He adds to this paramount theme in John 15:9, "Just as the Father has loved Me, I have also loved you; abide in My love." The next verse explains that the way to abide in His love is by obedience to His commandments. He continues to emphasize this same indispensable truth of a love relationship with Him in later verses (John 15:12–14, 17; 16:27).

From this brief overview of Jesus' last instructions to His disciples, it is plain to see that God's marvelous plan for His children is that they enjoy a wonderful, loving relationship with Him as their heavenly Father. Nowhere is it in the heart of God that the Christian life should be a burden to bear or a drudgery to endure or mere duties to be done. He purposes that we live a life saturated with His love (Ephesians 3:18–19, 5:1–2). He wants and has made every provision for you and me to enjoy our Christian life with Him with joy and peace (John 14:27, 15:11).

How can this be our experience?

Two fundamental issues must be settled in your heart if you are going to enjoy this kind of relationship with God. The first is this: You need to know deep inside that God loves you. He wants you to know this above all other knowledge. Everything, and I mean everything, from your flesh, the world, and the devil wages war against your relishing this astonishing good news. Echoing in every crevice of your soul and reverberating through your mind is the persistent thought, "I am not worthy. How could God really love me? I can never deserve it." The naked truth is that nothing about you, in you, or from you would cause God to love you. You are unworthy to the nth degree, and the first step to enjoying a loving relationship with God is to accept this fact. Nothing in you causes God to love you, nor is there anything that can cause God not to love you. Knowing the worst about you He loves you with a steadfast love and has loved you since before the world was ever made (Ephesians 1:4–5). God has loved you in spite of your sin (Ephesians 2:4; Romans 5:8). Your heavenly Father loves you *as much as* He loves His Son, Jesus Christ (John 17:23). God loves you dearly with tender love. The word used for love in John 16:27 is not the usual word for God's love (*agape*) but is the word for tender affection (*phileo*). Jesus

50

loves you as the Father loves Him (John 15:9). His love for you is from everlasting to everlasting, and it is absolutely unshakeable and unchangeable (Romans 8:31–39). His love (*agape* and *phileo*) seeks your highest good no matter the cost to Him, and it does not depend upon anything in you. He loves you because He is love and you are one of His dearly created ones. This is stirring and momentous knowledge! If His love for you is not real to you, then you can ask Him to work in you this wonderful assurance. And He will answer! Peace, rest, and joy will follow. He wants you to experience His love, as well as know it from His Word (John 14:21, Romans 5:5). He desires that His Word become dynamically alive and real in you through His Spirit so that His love is powerfully effective in your heart. I will speak more about this later.

When my dad was in the last weeks of his earthly life, my wife and I were able to spend three weeks with him and Mom through the Christmas holidays. We would read the Bible and pray. We would talk about heaven and listen to music. Often I was in tears when I left his room at night. How hard it was to see him so sick and frail, this dad whom I loved and who loved me.

On one occasion I went to see him alone. I knew the time was approaching to tell him good-bye. You never know how long a beloved sick one will linger, but Dad's life was getting weaker by the day. I bent over the rail of his bed to hug him. My eighty-five-year-old father, who had once been a robust, six-foot-tall, energetic, and vibrant man, was now so thin and frail and weak. Cancer is a terrible thief. As I hugged him, our cheeks together and our arms around one another, a father and his only child, we both cried. We knew our separation this side of heaven was coming soon. I said, "Dad, I am going to miss you so much, and I love you so much." He responded in an unusual way for my Dad. He hugged me, patted me on my back, and kissed me on my cheek multiple times. Then with crying and tears he said, "Son, I love you; I love you; I love you." This sacred moment and precious exchange of affection, this magnificent gift from God, I will always cherish.

Does your heavenly Father love you less than my Dad expressed to me? No! A thousand times no! He loves you infinitely more! With infinite, eternal, and unchangeable tenderness He loves you. With

His heavenly embrace He says, "My dearest child, I love you; I love you; I love you!"

The cross of Jesus is God saying, "I love you!" The resurrection of Christ is God saying, "I love you!" When He called you to Himself in repentance and faith, God was saying, "I love you!" When He cleansed you and made your body the temple of His Spirit, God was saying, "I love you!" By giving you eternal life and a place in heaven, God is saying, "I love you!" All that He does for you is God saying to you, "Forever I have loved you, and forever I will love you!" Brennan Manning has a wonderful statement, "I could more easily contain Niagara Falls in a tea cup than I can comprehend the wild, uncontainable love of God."[3]

The second issue, if you are going to experience a wonderful and enjoyable relationship with God, is this: Do you know deep in your heart that you love God? The whole basis of the Christian life is a love relationship with God as your Father, Jesus Christ as your Lord, and the Holy Spirit as your indwelling life. "We love because He first loved us" (1 John 4:19). Peter wrote, "Without having seen Him you love Him; though you do not [even] now see Him you believe in Him, and exult and thrill with inexpressible and glorious [triumphant, heavenly] joy" (1 Peter 1:8, AMP, brackets in original). We love Him out of gratitude for what He has done for us. However, we also love Him because we choose to love Him above all else. The Greek word Jesus used for loving Him is *agape*, the very same word used of God's love for us. *Agape* is not primarily a feeling love, a love of emotions, although emotions can become involved. It is a love of choice by one's will for another's highest good. It is willfully sacrificing self for another's best interest.

We are commanded in the greatest commandment to love God with all our heart, soul, and mind (Matthew 22:37). A command can be obeyed. Obedience occurs by a choice of one's will. Therefore, one who knows and has received God's love can respond by choosing to love God above all else. This means to put Him first in your life. It means to be completely submitted to Him in every area of your life so that He is sovereign Lord over your entire being. All that you have and all that you are is released to Him! Abandoned to Jesus with deep humility, you will lovingly and joyfully do whatever He bids you do.

Of course you are not left on your own to love God this way. When you give yourself to obey, the Holy Spirit comes to your aid to make it real within. You cannot love this way without Him. He readily enables you as soon as He has your permission by your choice to obey. He alone is the fountain of heavenly love that can flow through your soul like a river. This is life abundant that will make your life rich, full, and joyful (John 10:10). This does not mean life will be easy, free from struggles, trials, temptations, failures, and sorrows. Underneath and surrounding you like an ocean, however, will be a satisfying love relationship with your heavenly Father, and your Lord Jesus, who loves you and sacrificed Himself for you. This kind of relationship is the basis for the fullness of God's Spirit that He wants you to have.

Immediately preceding Jesus' declaration that He would ask the Father to give us another Helper, He states, "If you love me, you will keep my commandments" (John 14:15). Love for Christ leads to obedience to Christ. Jesus emphasizes a love relationship. Often when we think of obedience we think of it as drudgery. We think of it as having to do what we have no inspiration or pleasure to do. Obeying Jesus Christ is no more drudgery than dearly loving someone is drudgery. I dearly love my wife of forty-five years. Therefore it is my delight and joyful pleasure to serve her and take care of her. I cannot imagine coming home after a long trip away and thinking as the plane approaches the airport, "I suppose I have to go home to kiss my wife and take care of her." After all these years together, I still get excited, and my heart beats faster as the plane approaches the airport, and I anticipate seeing her and being with her. So it should be in our relationship with the Lord. With deep love for Him and knowing His deep love for us, it should be our joyful delight to obey Him. That is why John writes, "His commandments are not burdensome" (1 John 5:3). Love keeps them from being a burden.

The night before Jesus was crucified, Peter denied three times that he even knew Him. A few days later in a resurrection appearance by the sea Jesus had a penetrating conversation with Peter and asked, "Simon, son of John, do you love Me more than these?"

Jesus asked Peter this question three times (John 21:15–17). Jesus focused on the fundamental issue: "Do you love Me?" To the church in Ephesus Jesus said, "You have left your first love" (Revelation 2:4). The reason for their failure was their fall from their first love for Christ. Love is the melodious texture of all the Christian life. Paul Gerhardt (1607–1676) wrote:

> O grant that nothing in my soul
> >May dwell, but Thy pure love alone;
> O may Thy love possess me whole,
> >My joy, my treasure, and my crown:
> Strange fires far from my soul remove;
> May every act, word, thought, be love.[4]
> >>Tr. John Wesley (1703–1791)

If Jesus' life and ministry cannot be explained apart from the Holy Spirit, then how much more do I need the Spirit? I need Him in order to love God with all of my being. I need Him in order to love my wife Gerrie like Christ loves the Church. I need Him in order to be a father to my children like my heavenly Father. I need Him in order to be like Jesus to my grandchildren. I need Him in order to love my fellow Christians, especially difficult ones, and to have compassion for the lost. I need Him to intercede for me when I know not what, nor how, to pray. I need Him to comfort me when there is pain and distress in my soul. I need Him to encourage me when I have miserably failed by sin and am guilt-laden. I need Him to encourage me when discouragement by circumstances overshadows me like a solar eclipse.

The Holy Spirit, who is exactly like Jesus, has been given so you can experience the reality of Jesus' presence with you here and now. By His power you can enjoy your relationship with God, allowing the Holy Spirit to work out your conformity to the likeness of Jesus Christ, and accomplish His will for the sake of His kingdom and His honor.

My dear, loving heavenly Father,

What can I say before One so holy and pure as You? Nothing in me is worthy of Your loving compassion, and yet You love me with infinite, eternal, and tender love. Can I do less than give You all that I am and have, even though I know it is a sinful and imperfect gift? With all my heart I thank You for receiving me through Jesus Christ. Please lead me into all the fullness of Your Spirit. Help me to understand these truths so my life will honor and glorify You. Amen!

Notes

[1] Gerald F. Hawthorne, *The Presence and the Power*, (Dallas, London, Vancouver, Melbourne: Word Publishing, 1991), 35.

[2] J. I. Packer, *Keep in Step with the Spirit*, (Old Tappan, New Jersey: Fleming H. Revell Company, 1984), 55, 65–66.

[3] Brennan Manning, *The Ragamuffin Gospel*, (Sisters, Oregon: Multnomah Publishers, 1990, 2000), 162.

[4] Words of Paul Gerhardt quoted by A. W. Tozer, *The Christian Book of Mystical Verse*, (Harrisburg, Pennsylvania: Christian Publications, Inc., 1963), 66.

CHAPTER THREE

The Spirit Comes in Fullness

Satan has opposed the doctrine of the Spirit-filled life about as bitterly as any other doctrine there is. He has confused it, opposed it, surrounded it with false notions and fears. He has blocked every effort of the Church of Christ to receive from the Father her divine and blood-bought patrimony. The Church has tragically neglected this great liberating truth—that there is now for the child of God a full and wonderful and completely satisfying anointing with the Holy Ghost.
—A. W. Tozer, *How to Be Filled with the Holy Spirit*

I briefly told about my wife Gerrie's discovery of the Spirit's fullness in Chapter 1. With her quiet personality the Lord met her with His fullness in a quiet way. As her family we have watched her walk through heartaches, disappointments, sorrows, and happiness with steadiness, stability, and a quiet, gentle spirit. Those closest to you see clearest who you really are. She tells what made the difference in her life:

I became a Christian when I was a young girl in grade school. The most significant spiritual happening occurred when I came to understand about the filling of God's Holy Spirit. Before that time, my life was marked with fear and insecurity. To me, the Bible was just a book of empty words. As a wife and young mother, I was a great failure. I was desperate for God to give me the strength to obey Him. I began to see in God's Word that Jesus was to be my Lord, my Owner and Master. I understood that God's Spirit was holy and that because I was unclean on the inside, God's Spirit could not flow through me. So I dealt with the sins that God showed me, and as best as I understood, I was then in a place where my heart was clean. I quietly, and as a deliberate act of my will, knelt before God and verbally committed my whole life to the Lordship of Jesus Christ. I had a simple awareness that inside of my whole body, God's Spirit was filling me. The first difference I noticed was that when I would read God's Word, it was very personal and alive to me. Secondly, I began to notice that love was flowing from me to people around me, and I had nothing to do with it happening. I began to recognize the voice of the Shepherd as He led me each day. (John 10:27, "My sheep hear My voice.")

The first thing I heard Him tell me to do was to go make a pot of vegetable soup. I had never made vegetable soup before that morning. There were no plans in my day for anyone to come to visit my home. But I obeyed what I thought was the Holy Spirit speaking to me, and I made the soup. That afternoon my husband came home with a man and a woman that he had found on the street and they were hungry. We sat at the table and ate that soup.

One meaningful change in my life was that I knew peace in my heart. I lived those days, and I still live today, with this most wonderful realization inside of me. It is that the Holy Spirit indwells me and is my Teacher, my Counselor, and my Guide. When we live with The Teacher, The Counselor, and The Guide indwelling us, we do not have to live with fear or anxiety or insecurity. It is a wonderful gift that God has given.

Today, some thirty-plus years later, I have never lost the wonder of the truth that God indwells me by His Spirit. Yet I live almost everyday with the continuing awareness that in me there is no good thing.

I desire always to hear the voice of my Shepherd. The truth is I don't always hear correctly or obey perfectly. But Jesus has never failed to draw me back to Himself, restore my soul with the truth, and send me on my way with peace and joy and hope.

This wonderful gift God has given began with the first disciples on the day of Pentecost. Jesus told His disciples to wait until they were "clothed with power from on high" so that they could become His witnesses throughout the world (Luke 24:47–49, Acts 1:8). Jesus had made a few startling resurrection appearances to them, but now the disciples were in an interim of waiting for the Spirit to come. The Spirit would not be sent until Jesus was glorified (John 7:39). God set the day for the Spirit to be poured out on His children just as precisely as He set the day for His Son's birth, but the disciples did not know when that would happen. All they knew was that Jesus told them it would not be many more days until they would be baptized with or in the Holy Spirit (Acts 1:5). They must have wondered what this meant and what it would be like. How would this affect them? They waited "for the promise of the Father" (Acts 1:4) and knew that when the Spirit arrived they would receive God's power so necessary for becoming His witnesses wherever they went (Acts 1:8). The Spirit's arrival in fullness and anointing would cause their lives to be unexplainable just as the Spirit had caused Jesus' life to be unexplainable.

The First Disciples Filled

When the day of Pentecost came, the Father poured out His Spirit on the disciples gathered in a room. All of them were filled with the Holy Spirit. Supernatural signs accompanied the arrival of the Spirit, which validated His arrival, such as the sound of a mighty rushing wind filling the entire house where they were sitting, tongues as of fire appearing and resting on each of them, and speaking in other human languages as the Spirit gave them utterance (Acts 2:1–4).

Sometimes Christians focus on the supernatural signs that accompanied the initial outpouring of the Spirit rather than on the purpose of Jesus' promise. Do these supernatural events ever occur now? Sometimes they do because God in His omniscience chooses for them to happen to accomplish His own purposes. I know two Baptist men who spoke the good news in languages they had never learned. In Andrew Murray's church (Dutch Reformed, during the late eighteen hundreds) in South Africa, it was reported that the Holy Spirit came as a rushing, mighty wind and revival broke out. Supernatural events may occur in God's sovereign choice, but this is secondary rather than primary. We must be careful not to become fascinated with the supernatural and miss the real reason for the Holy Spirit being given.

The filling of the Spirit effected an inward change in the disciples. Men who ran in fear before the cross now stood in boldness after the Spirit came (Acts 2:22–23, 4:13–31). Feeble words of men became powerful words from heaven that cut to the heart (Acts 2:37). Ordinary men became mighty instruments in God's hand for the expansion of His kingdom throughout the pagan world (Acts 3:1–26). Instead of the Holy Spirit being given only to prophets, priests, and kings as in the Old Testament, He was given to every believer. Jesus, by the Holy Spirit, was with them and in them with all of His power wherever each of them went, something He could not do when He walked among them. This would make their lives and His church unexplainable and powerfully effective in its mission.

New Believers Filled

When Peter stood with the eleven disciples (Acts 2:14–36), all of whom were filled with the Spirit, he explained this strange phenomenon by citing the Old Testament prophet Joel from 2:28–32. He then proclaimed the gospel to the multitude that had gathered, and coming under conviction by the Spirit, they asked, "Brethren, what shall we do?" Peter responded, "Repent, and each of you be baptized in the name of Jesus Christ for the forgiveness of your sins, and *you will receive the gift of the Holy Spirit"* (Acts 2:37–38, italics added). Immediately, following the first sermon after the Spirit was poured out, Peter points these first converts to the fulfillment of messianic prophecy and the importance of the Holy Spirit for their new lives. Repentance, trust in Jesus, and baptism followed by receiving the gift of the Holy Spirit were the elements of Peter's message and invitation. A brief survey in Acts discloses that the Spirit's fullness was the norm for first-century Christians. It was an indispensable part of the whole Christian message and experience.

Philip was one of the seven chosen to help handle a problem that arose in the infant church (Acts 6:1–6). The apostles told the congregation to select seven men of good reputation, full of the Spirit and of wisdom. Philip was among those who had been filled with the Spirit. When the church was scattered because of persecution, Philip went to Samaria to proclaim the gospel to those whom the Jews were so prejudiced against. God confirmed the message with miraculous signs, and they received the Word of God (Acts 8:1–13). The report reached the apostles in Jerusalem, and Peter and John were sent to Samaria. When they arrived, Peter and John prayed for the Samaritan converts that they might receive the Holy Spirit and "they began laying their hands on them, and they were receiving the Holy Spirit" (Acts 8:14–17). Again we see the importance of the Holy Spirit for new converts, which the first church emphasized as fundamental for the Christian life. The Samaritans believing the Word, trusting Jesus, being baptized, and receiving the Spirit added convincing proof that salvation and the gift of the Spirit were for all believers everywhere.

The young man, Saul of Tarsus, despised the "new cult" of Jesus of Nazareth. Already a murderer of Christians, Saul was on a mission to annihilate the new church movement. His pursuit of believers took him on a journey from Jerusalem to Damascus (Acts 9:1–19). Nearing the city, he had a miraculous encounter with the resurrected Christ whom he despised. He was struck blind with a vision and a flash of light and was converted to Christ. His traveling companions took him into Damascus where he spent three days neither eating nor drinking. In a vision God spoke to Ananias to go and fulfill the vision God gave to Saul about a man named Ananias coming to lay hands on him and praying for him to receive his sight. Ananias went and prayed two things for Saul. He prayed for Saul to regain his sight. Then he prayed for Saul, this former persecutor only three days old in the Lord, to be filled with the Holy Spirit (Acts 9:17). It strikes me how seldom we in evangelical churches pray for new converts to be filled with the Holy Spirit after their conversion. The first-century church saw it to be essential for the normal Christian life. It was as much a part of the truth for them as repentance, faith in Christ, forgiveness, and baptism. Do we see it the same way?

God supernaturally directed the apostle Peter and a Gentile Roman centurion named Cornelius for an encounter that would bring the gospel to Cornelius and his entire household (Acts 10:1–48). As Peter proclaimed the Word of God to them, the gift of the Holy Spirit was poured out on Cornelius and his household (vv. 44–48) just as He was on the Jews on the day of Pentecost and on the Samaritans in Acts 8:4–17. This was additional convincing evidence that the gift of the Spirit knows no racial or cultural boundaries. Jews, Samaritans, and Gentiles alike partake of this wonderful and necessary heavenly Gift sent on the day of Pentecost.

On his second missionary journey, Paul went to Ephesus where he found some believers he thought were Christians (Acts 19:1–7). He must have recognized that there was something lacking in their experience because he asked them, "Did you receive the Holy Spirit when you believed?" (Acts 19:2). So crucial was the Holy Spirit for every Christian that this was his immediate concern when he sensed some deficiency in them. It turned out that they were believers in God who had only received John's baptism of repentance. They did not even know about the Holy Spirit because, although they were believers in God, they had not yet received the knowledge of Christ, and therefore had not come to faith in Him. Through Paul's teaching they came to faith in Christ and were baptized. When Paul laid hands on them, the Holy Spirit came on them with the same convincing proof that was given in Samaria and Cornelius' house. The early church needed to understand clearly that the Spirit was equally for every new convert. God confirmed this fact again and again as He poured out His Spirit on believers of every race and social position across Asia, Europe, and northern Africa.

If Paul could visit our churches today, would he sense the same lack as in these Ephesians and ask, "Did you receive the Holy Spirit when you believed?" He could not have been talking about the indwelling of the Spirit because that is what distinguishes a Christian from a non-Christian (Romans 8:9). He must have been referring to the fullness of the Spirit. To personalize the question, "Did you receive the fullness of the Spirit when you trusted Christ?" What if you could ask Peter or Paul or Stephen or Philip or any of the first-century Christians, "Do you remember when you were first filled with the Holy Spirit?" What do you think their response would be? Of course it would be an emphatic yes, and they could tell you when and where. If they returned the question to you about when and where you were first filled with the Spirit, what would be your response?

James Gilchrist Lawson wrote, "Most of the great Bible scholars and commentators, and most of the great church historians are agreed upon the fact it was the custom of the early church to pray for all believers to be filled with the Spirit. The usual custom was to baptize the converts, and then the elders would lay hands on them and pray for them to receive the gift of the Holy Ghost."[1] He also wrote, "The early Christian church believed in and prayed for the filling of the Holy Spirit, and this was the secret of its power."[2] He referred to early Christian writers, both the Greek and Roman Fathers of the Church and said that they "testify to the fact that in the second century and later, it was customary to pray for Christians to be filled with the Spirit, just as they were prayed for in Bible times."[3] He verifies this by quoting several church historians from the second and third centuries.

From the book of Acts there are four clear observations we can make about the work of the Holy Spirit in believers:

1. The fullness of the Holy Spirit is a gift from God.
2. The fullness of the Holy Spirit is a distinct and definite reality.
3. The fullness of the Holy Spirit is clearly evident.
4. The fullness of the Holy Spirit produces certain results.

Is Satan's opposition, as mentioned in the quote by Tozer at the beginning of this chapter, the reason many evangelical Christians have ignored and retreated from the correct biblical and early-church position of the necessity for the Holy Spirit's fullness in every believer beginning with their conversion and baptism? Shall we grieve the Spirit by neglecting this Gift because of extremisms and wrong emphases that we have seen or heard about in some professing Christian circles? If our desire is to honor the Christ whom we love, then should we not receive from Him all He has purchased for us and provided for us as free gifts? Shall we refuse so costly a gift?

Continual Fullness with the Spirit

Some first believers who had been filled with the Spirit lived continually in a state of fullness. Dr. Luke, used by the Spirit to author Acts, carefully testified to this by several examples.

Discontent and complaints arose in the first-century church from the Greek-speaking Jews against the Hebrew-speaking Jews. They thought their widows were being discriminated against in the distribution of the food. The apostles knew they must give themselves to prayer and the ministry of God's Word, and they should not be distracted by this practical task of food distribution. They explained this to the church and told them, "Therefore, brethren, select from among you seven men of good reputation, *full of the Spirit* and of wisdom, whom we may put in charge of this task" (Acts 6:3, italics added). The church approved the plan and seven men meeting the stated qualifications were appointed. The church wisely chose men with Greek names.

In order for the church to choose men full of the Holy Spirit, there had to be an observable trait. There was a quality about Spirit-filled men that distinguished them from those lacking the Spirit's fullness. My son and I were discussing this at lunch together one day, and he humorously put it, "God might as well have said, 'Pick out the purple people.' It would have been that obvious."

Stephen is another example of a man continuously full of the Holy Spirit (Acts 6:5, 7:55). God used him to proclaim the truth about Jesus and confirmed it with signs and wonders. Some religious Jews argued with Stephen, but they could not cope with the wisdom the Spirit gave him. Therefore they dragged him away and put him on trial before the Jewish Council. He was falsely charged with speaking blasphemous words (Acts 6:11–14). Before the council, his face was like the face of an angel (Acts 6:15). No doubt the fullness of God's Spirit affected his countenance so that the light of Christ shone through. He explained his position and charged the council with resisting the Spirit and disobeying God's Word just like their forefathers had done. The religious leaders became infuriated. Dr. Luke records, "But *being full of the Holy Spirit*, he gazed intently into heaven and saw the glory of God, and Jesus standing at the right hand of God" (Acts 7:55, italics added).

Another illustration of continuous fullness is Barnabas. The Word states, "He was a good man, and *full of the Holy Spirit* and of faith" (Acts 11:24, italics added). In another place Luke states, "The disciples *were continually filled with joy and with the Holy Spirit*" (Acts 13:52, italics added).

The Apostle Paul wrote a letter to the church in Ephesus that began on his second missionary journey in Acts 19:1–7. In this letter, he wrote for them to keep on being filled with the Spirit (Ephesians 5:18). The Greek verb means "be continuously filled." In other words, "always live in a state of the Spirit's fullness." This command is totally unnecessary if every believer is automatically and always filled with the Spirit. These Ephesian believers remembered when they were initially filled during Paul's first visit, and now the apostle commands them to continue in the state of the Spirit's fullness.

Initial filling by the Spirit should be followed by continual fullness with the Spirit.

Fullness of the Spirit Defined

You may be asking, "What is the fullness of the Holy Spirit? What does it mean to be filled with the Spirit?"

The fullness of the Holy Spirit is a relationship with the indwelling third Person of the Trinity whereby He is permitted to exercise His holy influence over every area of your life. The result is the fruit of Christ-likeness revealed through your personality. This beautiful effect increases as you mature spiritually. Fullness by the Spirit releases God's power in you so that by His strength and energy you can live and minister. (Ministry includes every manner of service in the Name of Christ regardless of how insignificant it seems in the eyes of men.) Love, joy, peace, patience, kindness, goodness, faithfulness, gentleness, and self-control become descriptive of the kind of person you are (Galatians 5:22–23). The life in the vine, which is Jesus, becomes the fruit in the branch, which is you (John 15:1–11). The rivers Jesus promised to flow from your inner being come forth to refresh others around you, beginning with your family (John 7:37–38). The flow may be small at first, but as you mature spiritually, the size of the rivers of living water flowing out of you will increase. Others are able to catch glimpses of Jesus who indwells you and fills you with His Spirit. I have been with some in whom I sensed the very presence of Jesus because they were so full of Him. They had walked with Him in fullness for many years and the rivers flowing from their inner being were deep and wide. It is always encouraging, refreshing, challenging, and convicting to be with such dear believers. As the tree is full of sap, and the sun is full of light, and the spring in fullness overflows with refreshing, cool water, so your life can be full to overflowing with the Spirit of Christ.

The alternative is fullness of self expressed through self-will, self-seeking, self-pleasing, self-confidence, and self-exaltation ruling your heart. Instead of the beauty of Christ, the ugliness of the flesh's works are expressed in your life—things like selfish attitudes, selfish motives, selfish words, selfish deeds, and selfish neglect of the good you should have done. Like the moon eclipsing the sun, so your self-life eclipses the One who lives in you. Your life can be quite good, sincere, and moral—even used to some degree by God—but you lack the added dimension that only comes from the Spirit's fullness. You have not received all God wants to give you, and Jesus is not glorified in you like God has intended. This is a terrible loss and waste, both for you and also for the honor and glory of Christ.

Contemporary Believers Filled

Dr. Gerald F. Hawthorne wrote, "There is no reason whatsoever to believe that what was true of those earliest Christians is any less true of Christians in this century . . . God's program of enabling people to burst the bounds of their human limitations and achieve the impossible is still in place and still effective. That program involves filling people with His Spirit, filling them with supernatural power."[4]

A. W. Tozer wrote, "The Spirit-filled life is not a special, deluxe edition of Christianity. It is part and parcel of the total plan of God for His people. You must be satisfied that it is not abnormal. I admit that it is unusual, because there are so few people who walk in the light of it or enjoy it, but it is not abnormal. In a world where everybody was sick, health would be unusual, but it wouldn't be abnormal."[5]

B. H. Carroll, known as the "Colossus of Baptist History" (1843–1914) and founder of Southwestern Baptist Theological Seminary in Fort Worth, Texas, wrote: "I speak of a blessing of God entirely distinct from and subsequent to your penitence and your faith. I speak not of regenerating grace that makes you a child of God, but I speak of a glory that comes to you because you are a child of God, and I solemnly press upon your hearts with all possible emphasis today—have you received the Holy Spirit since you believed? If you have not, that is what is the matter with you; that explains your weakness; that tells why you limp as you walk and stammer as you talk. That accounts for your lack of power and joy; that explains why it is that clouds shut out from your sight the smiling face of God."[6]

H. E. Dana, a Greek scholar, wrote, "No one can read carefully and thoughtfully the book of Acts without experiencing the general impression that the state of 'being filled with the Spirit' is viewed as the normal and necessary state of Christian experience . . . The apostles recognized no life as fully qualified in the kingdom without this blessing . . . At any rate, we believe this record makes it unmistakably clear that the infilling of the Spirit came to these disciples as a blessing distinct from salvation, and that these Christians were not considered as having attained a rightful and normal experience until this blessing had been received."[7]

Many other quotes could be added from evangelical scholars and leaders affirming the same truth. Any of us must come to the same conclusion by a careful reading of the book of Acts. In Acts and from the testimonies of contemporary Christians, you will notice that there is no standard way for believers to enter the Spirit's fullness. As a young man hungry for more than I knew in my Christian life, I thought I had to have some dramatic experience like I read about in biographies of famous Christians. I learned that is not true. There is no standard for experience. The Lord with tender love deals with each of His children in a unique and personal way. You cannot have another's experience. To think you must leads to frustration, disappointment, and discouragement, or worse yet, a counterfeit experience. It causes you to ask, "What is wrong with me?"

Some receive the Spirit's fullness in a quiet manner while others may have an experience or feeling when they are filled. Some enter fullness while praying alone, but sometimes it helps to have someone pray with the one who is seeking the Spirit's fullness. Like in the book of Acts, there is no set pattern.

Last summer a team of us went to Japan to give the missionaries, pastors, and Christian workers of International Chapel Ministries a retreat to encourage and hopefully refresh them. These workers have demanding schedules and work tirelessly in a difficult culture of many gods. They faithfully seek to evangelize some from the one hundred twenty-seven million who are engulfed in the darkness of paganism and need to know about Jesus. By means of chapels (churches) they have established, they reach out to the lost and shepherd those who come to Christ.

On the last day of the retreat we had a service centered on the Lord's Supper. The retreat had been meaningful for all of us, and this was a fitting way to conclude. We had two tables at the front on either side with the communion elements on each table. I stood at the table on the right and another man on our team stood at the table on the left. Each one was to come individually, those on the right to me and those on the left to Mark. An interpreter stood beside each of us to translate for those who could not speak English. We spoke personal words of encouragement to each of them and then served them the Lord's Supper.

Towards the end of the group of those who came to my table was a young Japanese woman. As she stood there before me I had this inner urge to pray for her, which I had not done for the others. I did not know who she was. Although I had seen her, I had no knowledge of her. So after serving her the Lord's Supper, I prayed, and Junko, standing beside me, interpreted. She was the only one I was impressed to pray for this way. Two things came to mind to pray. I asked the Lord to set her free from anything that bound her and to fill her with His Spirit. A couple of days later I learned that she is a Japanese pastor's wife and just what the Lord had done in her life. Here is Tomoko's testimony:

> It has been thirteen years since I became a Christian. For many of those years, I experienced severe mood swings, and once I went into deep depression, and it was very hard for me to come out of it. Also, I had problems relating to others. I was always thinking, "What are they thinking about me? What will people think of me if I say this?" So it was very hard for me to show others the real me. For this reason, whenever I spoke to those over me, chapel staff members or those who spoke English (or such people who spoke to me first), I was filled with fear. In addition, I had quite an inferiority complex, and even when my husband or others complimented me, I still considered myself to be inferior.

About three years ago, when Mr. White came to chapel to speak for the first time, he spoke about the ministry of the Holy Spirit. At that time, I read one after another of the books about the Holy Spirit that he had recommended to my husband, and I began to pray earnestly that I would be 'filled with the Holy Spirit.' Last year, in April, I went through a particularly difficult time when I wondered if I could even continue in the Christian life. I came to realize profoundly that I was completely without the filling of the Holy Spirit, and I continued to pray seriously that I could receive the Holy Spirit.

When I heard that Mr. White and the others would be coming to Japan again in August, I felt depressed. The reason for this is that I wondered if I, who cannot speak English, would ever be able to enjoy the meetings. Moreover, when I thought about the fact that there would be many English-speaking people coming who were unknown to me, it made me even more depressed. But the Lord knew everything I was feeling and thinking, and He began to work in my heart even before the meetings began. A few weeks before the seminar, I received an unexpected e-mail from a sister on the team. Through that e-mail, the Lord gave me clear guidance that I should attend the seminar, even though I had had no desire to do so. During the seminar, God spoke resoundingly in my heart. Even so, I couldn't shake the doubts about whether the Lord would take away my fear and sense of inferiority.

Also, when I heard that we were going to partake of the Lord's Supper at the end of the seminar, I hesitated, wondering if it was all right for me to receive it in my present condition. In the end, I decided to attend.

While I was standing before Mr. White after partaking of the bread and grape juice, he prayed for

me, 'Lord, fill her with Your Spirit and release her
from anything that binds her.' I didn't feel anything
change at the time, but the next day, my morning devo-
tions were unlike anything I had ever experienced
before! I no longer had any doubts, and for the first
time I felt very deeply that God was there with me. I
stopped viewing the things people did and said to me
negatively. Also, I am no longer poor at getting along
with others, but, rather, I am now able to love people
from my heart. I am so surprised at the change in me.
I had often felt that I had considerable demonic problems as a result of my past miserable family situation
(my father's violent behavior, alcoholism, the enmity
between my parents, etc.) but when I was filled with
the Holy Spirit, the Lord completely delivered me
from all the demonic strongholds in my life. He
knew all that I had suffered through . . . I have come
to know how wonderful it is to live in the Lord by
the power of the Holy Spirit, and I am determined to
keep my eyes on the Lord as I walk with Him so that
I will never lose the fullness of the Spirit.

Tomoko's prayers asking God to fill her with His Spirit were
answered in a wonderful and unexpected way. At the moment we
prayed neither of us was aware of any special touch by the Lord.

Some have dramatic encounters with the Lord Jesus without
anyone assisting them when they are filled with His Spirit. Many
years ago I counseled a man at a conference where I was the guest
speaker. Years later I learned about the miraculous work God did in
his life apart from any counseling. Bobby Dixon tells his story:

Early one Friday morning in Vidalia, Georgia on
December 5, 1975, my wife and I boarded a church
bus en route to a couples' retreat being held at Park
Avenue Baptist Church in Titusville, Florida. We
were not Christians, had never attended a retreat of

any kind, had been separated for seventeen months, and divorce papers had been filed.

A prayer group had been praying for us for two years. The fact we were on the bus was a visible expression of answered prayer.

Peter Lord, pastor of Park Avenue Church, was away that weekend ministering in another location, but the leader that he is, he had his team of people in place. Jerry White was the key speaker along with Cecil McGee, Danny Daniels, and Bill Flanders. We were ministered to at our point of need. We "heard" the gospel of Jesus Christ for the first time. Deliverance was accomplished in our lives and the people were so full of the love of Jesus we could not help but be overwhelmed by the Lord's presence.

Nothing tangible happened to us at the retreat and, as we learned later, the bus headed for home carrying heavy hearts. But God was not finished. On the way to Vidalia, in the third seat from the rear on the left-hand side, God reached down and dramatically changed my life.

The presence of Jesus was so strong I reached up my hand to touch Him. Of course, this was not physically, but in my mind. He was right there. I told Him I had made a mess of my life and would He please straighten me out. He took over as Lord of my life; forgave me of all my sins and set me free. I was filled to overflowing with the Holy Spirit and began to sing and praise Him. I embraced His forgiveness and walked in it. By the way, I call myself the second greatest sinner, Paul being the first. My wife had been saved earlier that day but remained quiet about it.

That very night I went home and was reunited with my wife and three children. Then God began our transformation! We were surrounded by folks who loved the Lord and discipled us. We had a steady diet of preaching tapes for lunch, at night, and at the home meetings we attended. By this we learned about the Christian walk—forgiveness, authority, you must "be" before you "do," submission, sovereignty of God, and who I am in Christ.

God moved me from being an automobile dealer and lumber manufacturer to being involved with my wife in a full-time marriage and family-counseling ministry, Christian Concepts for Living. Hundreds have come to Christ through this ministry over the years. I am now an ordained minister and pastor of a Presbyterian Church.

Our lives are full and running over with the goodness of the Lord Jesus Christ.

Our Lord meets spiritually thirsty people with His blessing in His own perfect and all-wise will. In the next chapter we will look at the simple way you can enter into the fullness of the Holy Spirit. Before we do some questions are in order:

- Have you been filled with the Spirit? If not, what has kept you from it?
- Have you not understood its necessity and God's gracious provision for the fullness of the Holy Spirit?
- Have you been afraid of it because of extremisms you have seen or heard about?
- Have you doubted the reality of this doctrine for modern Christians?
- Have you not believed God would give you this gift?
- Have you felt too unworthy to receive the gift of His fullness?
- Have you known fullness of the Spirit before but lost it through carelessness in your relationship with Christ?
- Are you now at a place where you want to enter the fullness of the Spirit God longs to give you?

L. L. Legters wrote, "The heart of God can never be satisfied until He fills us with the Holy Spirit. Our hearts will never be satisfied except as we are filled with the Holy Spirit. Let us remember that it is the heart longing of God that we be filled."[8]

Sovereign loving Father,

There is no way I can adequately express my gratitude to You for salvation by the cross of Christ. You and You alone brought me from death to life, forgave me, and gave me Your own righteousness as a gift. Then with full knowledge of my utter weakness, You gave me the gift of Your Spirit so that I can live in the power of Your resurrection Life indwelling and filling me. Thank You that more than I want to be filled You want to fill me with all Your fullness. Please show me the way so that my whole life can be lived saturated with You. Amen!

Notes

[1] J. Gilchrist Lawson, *Deeper Experiences of Famous Christians*, (Anderson, Indiana: The Warner Press, 1922), 44.

[2] Ibid., 46.

[3] Ibid., 50.

[4] Hawthorne, *The Presence and the Power*, 238.

[5] A. W. Tozer, *How to be Filled with the Holy Spirit*, (Harrisburg, Pennsylvania: Christian Publications, Inc.), 18–19.

[6] From a pamphlet by Mrs. Rosalee Mills Appleby, *Testimonies of Famous Christians Concerning the Filling and Baptism of the Holy Spirit*, (Lubbock, Texas: Missionary Crusader).

[7] Ibid.

[8] L. L. Legters, *The Simplicity of the Spirit-filled Life*, (Hempstead, Long Island, New York: Service and Supplies for Christian Work, Inc., 1930, 1952), 32.

CHAPTER FOUR

The Way to Receive Fullness

The great heart of God is longing to fill you with His Spirit. God is yearning over you, beyond the thought of man to express, to fill you with His fullness . . . We forget that God is a giving God; that God delights to give His Holy Spirit; that God is seeking to fill us with His Spirit.

—L. L. Legters, *The Simplicity of the Spirit-Filled Life*

A few summers ago I spoke at a conference at The Evangelical Institute in Greenville, South Carolina. Thursday night's message was about God's love being an experienced reality in one's life. This prepared the way for Friday night's message about being filled with the Holy Spirit. At the conclusion it seemed appropriate to give opportunity for any who had never been filled, or those who needed a fresh filling, to come kneel at the front for prayer. The whole front of the auditorium filled up with people, young and old, wanting to enter into fullness. As soon as I invited them to come, I noticed a middle-aged man quickly grab a chair and sit in the center as near the platform as he could. The next morning he gave

75

testimony as to what happened to him. A few weeks later he called me to further update me on what had occurred in his life as a result of that Friday night. Joseph, who has a prison ministry in Ohio where he lives, wrote:

> Off and on for twelve to fourteen years I had wanted the fullness of the Spirit but had never been able to enter in. Even though I had sought it by reading books, and hearing many messages on it, I did not understand how it could be mine. I had told the men in my prison ministry that I believed in it but I had never experienced it, though I desired to. A few days before attending the conference, I had gotten out the little booklet, "Victory in Christ" by Dr. Robert C. McQuilken, former President of Columbia Bible College, and I remember crying out to God after failing and falling to a particular sin again, "Does anyone walk in victory, Lord Jesus? Can anyone live this way? Because I know I'm not."
>
> I arrived at the conference physically, mentally, and spiritually spent. A few months before coming I fought back at least three times what I felt were the beginnings of a nervous breakdown. So I guess I was ready to give up, or maybe I'd already given up, I really don't know. What I do know is that coming to the conference to seek the fullness of the Spirit was the furthest thing from my mind. From the first day I sensed the Lord's presence. At the close of the Friday evening message, Pastor White gave an invitation for those who wanted to come forward to enter into the fullness of the Spirit by faith. I immediately went forward, grabbed a chair, brought it up to the altar, sat down (because I can't kneel), and just waited. Jerry said we needed to know and understand that Jesus wanted to put His arms around us and love us. When I asked the Lord Jesus to do that, I sensed a warmth and a presence I've never experienced before, and

tears came to my eyes. This is significant because I'm not an emotional person. Then Jerry walked us through some steps and led us in prayer to receive God's fullness by faith, which I did. In the steps Jerry was leading us through, he said that if there were sins the Lord was bringing to our minds we should deal with them right there, but if sins came to mind that we had already confessed, we should not be bothered by those. The Lord brought to my mind two men I needed to go back to and ask for their forgiveness because of how I had treated them. One of them was my pastor. We have never been really close. As a matter of fact, we would shake hands at church, greeting one another, but that is about as far as it ever went. For at least seven years, every time I went into church, I would have such anger in my spirit over how I had been treated in this church. This was to the point where for the last few years I have not been able to sing in church because of the emotional turmoil I was going through. When we got back Sunday from the conference, we went to church, and I sought out my pastor and asked if I could talk to him. He said yes, and we went into his office to speak privately. I simply told him that I had not been as supportive of him as I should have, not talking badly about him, but not giving him the support that he deserved. I asked for his forgiveness and he simply replied, "Consider yourself forgiven." He then got up from his desk and we hugged each other like we meant it. This is significant because I'm not a hugging person. At that point, however, I didn't mind giving my pastor a hug. When I went back to sit with my wife, all of a sudden it dawned on me that the great anger and emotional struggle was gone, even though I never asked God to take it away. I found myself singing in church for the first time in years.

I would like to point out that the fullness of the Spirit is not a feeling; it's much more. It's a sense of the Lord's presence that no words can describe.

The Path to Fullness

You may receive the Spirit's fullness quite simply! Trusting your heavenly Father like a child you can receive as easily as drinking! If your heart is ready, you can rest in the fact that your Father is ready to give you His fullness. Legters was right when he wrote, "The great heart of God is longing to fill you with His Spirit."[1] You need not beg, or plead, or be good enough. You may not have known that this wondrous gift has been yours since your conversion as a part of your salvation. In Acts the early Christians received the Spirit's fullness at their conversion or soon thereafter. God intends His fullness to be a normal part of the salvation experience. Many who come to Christ, however, do not know about this gift from the Father. Some time later they may learn about it, and then they go through a crisis-like experience in order to appropriate the fullness they could have had from the beginning had they only known about it. Others live their entire Christian lives and never enter the Spirit's fullness. Like the children of Israel they are delivered from the bondage of Egypt but eventually die in the wilderness without ever entering Canaan, the promised land of abundance God provided for them. They go to heaven, but, sadly, they missed out on all their loving Father longed to give to them during their earthly pilgrimage. It can be different for you. You can receive all the fullness of God's Spirit and live in the full blessing of God the rest of your earthly days. We now consider how any believer can receive the fullness of the Holy Spirit.

When Jesus spoke about the Spirit in John 7:37–39, He used three words in His invitation: Thirst—come—drink. What does each word mean?

Thirst! Thirst is need, desire, and even craving. Physically this speaks of a feeling of dryness in the mouth and throat that results in a desire or need for water. While dying on the cross Jesus said, "I thirst!" Water is the most basic need of the human body along with air to breathe. The stronger your thirst becomes the more determined you become to find whatever will quench it.

The Expository Dictionary of Bible Words says, "Famine and drought were among the most feared calamities of biblical times. Hunger and thirst represent humanity's most basic needs for survival. In a culture that saw God as the central reality, it is not surprising to find hunger and thirst linked in a number of ways with God.

In the material realm, God is looked to as the source of food and drink . . . Hunger and thirst are extended in Scripture to represent basic spiritual needs that also require satisfaction."[2] Psalm 42:2 speaks about spiritual thirst, "My soul thirsts for God, for the living God." Jesus was speaking of spiritual thirst in John 7:37. Spiritual thirst is a sense of dryness in the soul that results in a craving, which only God can satisfy.

The path to fullness with the Holy Spirit begins with spiritual thirst. This is what Jesus meant when He said, "If anyone is thirsty." Often Christians are so full of other things they do not thirst for God. Jeremiah wrote, "For My people have committed two evils: / They have forsaken Me, / The fountain of living waters, / To hew for themselves cisterns, / Broken cisterns that can hold no water" (Jeremiah 2:13). The world's cisterns never satisfy spiritual thirst. Only God's presence and His fullness can satisfy the deep longing of a regenerate soul. Spiritual thirst is when you deeply and profoundly know your need for the Spirit's fullness just like your parched mouth knows its need for water. Trying to satisfy your life with other things prevents you from drinking living water, and therefore, you don't experience the quality of Christian life God intends for all believers.

One of the saddest verses in the Bible is Psalm 106:20, "They exchanged the glory of God for the image of an ox that eats grass" (ESV). Do Christians not do the same today? We hold on to sexual immorality and give up the glory of God. We hold on to some personal privilege and give up the glory of God. We hold on to some secret sin or some wrong attitude and give up the glory of God. We cherish some earthly possession, or cling to some self-indulgence, or try to satisfy ourselves with the polluting selfishness of the world and give up the glory of God. Holding to these things nullifies your thirst for God's fullness. When once you realize that drinking from the world's cisterns never truly satisfies, you then will realize that you are robbing yourself of God's very best. If you thirst for God's fullness above all else, you are in a wonderful place. You may not have known to identify your desire as thirst for the fullness of the Spirit, but you have known something was lacking in your spiritual life. You have become aware of a need for something more in your relationship with Christ. If you do not thirst preeminently for God's fullness, you can humbly ask Him to cause you to thirst spiritually, and He will.

Come! This means come to Jesus, the ever-living and present Christ. Just as needy ones came to Jesus when He walked in the flesh, so with your impoverished soul come to Him. Come in the same manner that you came to Him in your lost condition needing salvation. Come as one helpless, knowing your bankruptcy without Him. Come in humility and honesty like a child. Come in prayer and faith. Come with your specific need to Him who loves you immeasurably. Come to the One who eagerly waits for you. If you could see His eyes looking at you, you would realize His vast compassion; understand that He longs to meet you in your need. He patiently waits for you to come.

Drink! One drinks by believing (John 7:37–38). All the promised blessings of God come through faith. Jesus always responds to those who have faith. God says that without faith it is impossible to please Him (Hebrews 11:6). The children of Israel could not enter the land of promise, even though they had God's promise, because the word spoken to them was not "united by faith in those who heard it" (Hebrews 4:2). Believing what God says and trusting Him to do exactly what He says is the nature of faith. When God—who cannot lie—makes a promise, we receive its fulfillment by trusting for it. Trust is willfully and actively believing God with mind and heart to keep His Word. Trust finds expression by pursuing God in prayer about a specific promise in His Word. Generations ago some believers called it "pleading the promises." This means holding God's promises before Him in prayer. You cling to His faithfulness and express confidence that He will keep His Word. This pleases Him because it honors His character. It says resoundingly, "I love You and trust You because I know You are faithful, and I wait expectantly for You to keep Your promise."

How does one drink? Drinking is not difficult. Infants instinctively know how to drink, even from birth. We drink by believing. We receive by believing. We trust Him to keep His promise. We fasten our souls to His promise and continue trusting Him to fulfill His Word. If it does not happen at once, we continue trusting until we have the assurance of God's answer. We do not look for evidence or experience. We please and honor Him by simply believing what He says. In prayer we confess His promise with thanksgiving and express our confidence in Him. This is what Abraham did regarding God's stunning promise to him. Romans 4:20 encourages us, "Yet, with respect to the promise of God, he [Abraham] did not waver in unbelief but grew strong in faith, giving glory to God."

Do not compare your experience of the Holy Spirit with anyone else's. Paul came to Christ in a very dramatic encounter (Acts 9:1–9), but Lydia came to salvation in a quieter way (Acts 16:11–15). It is the same with receiving God's fullness. Receiving fullness ushers you into a special kind of relationship with the Spirit. In the context of this intimate relationship you will have experiences according to God's sovereign choice, but they will be uniquely yours and not like anyone else's.

The present tenses (imperatives and participle) in John 7:37–38 indicate we keep on coming to Him, we keep on drinking, and we continue believing. Jesus then promises that out of our inner beings will continually flow rivers of living water. John gives a word of explanation in verse 39 about the meaning of living waters. Jesus was speaking of the Spirit who was going to be given when Jesus was glorified by His resurrection and enthronement in heaven. Satisfying our thirst by drinking of His fullness enables us to be spiritual refreshment for others. Our overflow will be rivers of love, joy, and peace.

Hindrances to Fullness

If fullness by the Spirit is a gift from the Father, then can anything hinder you from receiving this magnificent gift? The answer is yes. Two unsettled issues in your life can hinder reception of fullness.

Full Surrender Is Necessary

Holding back in some area of your life can hinder you from receiving fullness. True faith is giving up everything in order to follow Jesus. Jesus said, as He taught about the kingdom of heaven, "Again, the kingdom of heaven is like a merchant seeking fine pearls, and upon finding one pearl of great value, he went and sold all that he had and bought it" (Matthew 13:45–46). The merchant wanted that fine pearl so much he gladly gave up all he had to get it without any regrets. His focus was not on his great loss, but rather on his great gain. J. Oswald Sanders wrote in *Enjoying Intimacy with God*, "Sacrifice is the ecstasy of giving the best we have to the One we love the most."[3] Giving all to Christ without any reservation is nothing compared to what is gained for your life and His honor.

On another occasion Jesus said, "So then, none of you can be My disciple who does not give up all his own possessions" (Luke 14:33). In Matthew 19:27, Peter said, "Behold, we have left everything and followed You." On the day of Pentecost when the Spirit came profusely upon the disciples and filled them, He came upon those wholly His. All they were and possessed belonged to Christ because they had gladly bowed to His Lordship. This does not mean they walked perfectly never faltering. The Bible is quite honest about their failures. Your heart can be wholly His even though at times you stumble in your walk. James wrote in his letter, "We all stumble in many ways" (James 3:2).

Jesus lived in complete surrender to His Father. The disciples lived in complete surrender to Jesus. The apostle Paul considered himself Christ's love slave. The early disciples did not consider their lives their own and many willingly died in the Roman arenas for the love of Christ. Ignatius of Antioch wrote between AD 98 and AD 117 while a prisoner of Emperor Trajan, "Let me be food for the wild beasts—those in the stands and those in the arena! Offering my life in this way is not death to me. I lose nothing and gain eternal life in God. I am the wheat of God. If I am ground by the teeth of wild beasts I will be found in the pure bread of Christ."[4] Spectators in Rome's coliseum watched for their afternoon's pleasure as the wild beasts tore Ignatius apart. Ignatius was abandoned to Christ. Is that not what Jesus wants from all of us?

Oswald Chambers says, "The greatest word of Jesus to His disciples is ABANDON" (Chambers' emphasis). He also says, "To fulfill God's perfect design for me requires my total surrender—complete abandonment of myself to Him."[5] Abandonment means to give up control of your life by surrendering everything to Christ's control so that you do not claim any rights for yourself. It means willfully and entirely bowing to His Lordship so that you are wholly His to do with as He pleases. You become Christ's bondservant and forsake your selfish desires and plans by willfully choosing to live only for His will and honor. In decisive prayer you commit all you know of yourself to all you know of Him, and with glad confidence put your life entirely in the hands of Perfect Love. He has loved you before the universe was ever formed (Romans 8:29), and He loves you this moment beyond what you can imagine. His love for you is infinite, eternal, and pure. With full knowledge of the very worst about you, He loves you with all that He is. His perfect knowledge of your worst does not lessen His astounding love for you.

J. Wilbur Chapman (1859–1918) wrote, "The step has already been indicated. It is this: SURRENDER FULLY [Chapman's emphasis]. To give up ninety-nine parts of the nature and withhold the hundredth is to put a hindrance in the way of the blessing. If a contagious disease had been raging in a certain house, and you had a desire to live in the house, you know that you would not do it until every room had been purified. If every room but one had been fumigated, and that the smallest room, you know that you would not occupy the house. Nor will the Holy Spirit work with power in the life till it has been surrendered to him, till it has all been made clean by true confession: then make ready for the blessing which God has promised."[6]

A Clear Conscience Is Necessary

The second issue that can hinder your reception of the Spirit's fullness is having your conscience stained by sin. Ephesians 4:30 commands, "Do not grieve the Holy Spirit of God, by whom you were sealed for the day of redemption." Grief is a love word. A loved one's death causes grief because it brings loss and separation. The verses surrounding the verse above reveal the cause of grief to the

Spirit—sin. Sin makes the Holy Spirit sad, and if we desire His fullness we must understand that when the Spirit is grieved He cannot fill the one who grieves Him.

The Spirit grieves for two reasons. First, He grieves because He loves Jesus Christ and knows that Jesus is not being glorified through you like He should be. In addition, intimate fellowship between Christ and His child is interrupted. Christ is prevented from close fellowship with you, and He cannot empower you as He wants to because of excused or tolerated sin.

The second reason the Spirit grieves is because your close fellowship with Christ is lost. The Spirit knows that excused or tolerated sin robs you of the blessing Jesus wants to pour out on you, and through you to others. Isaiah proclaimed, "Behold, the Lord's hand is not so short / That it cannot save; / Nor is His ear so dull / That it cannot hear. But your iniquities have made a separation between you and your God, / And your sins have hidden His face from you so that He does not hear" (Isaiah 59:1–2).

What should you do if you have grieved the Spirit? Our heavenly Father understood this would happen and made full provision with instruction for what we should do. Sin must be dealt with honestly. Proverbs 28:13 says, "He who conceals his transgressions will not prosper, / But he who confesses and forsakes them will find compassion." David wrote, "When I kept silent about my sin, my body wasted away / Through my groaning all day long . . . I acknowledged my sin to You, / And my iniquity I did not hide; / I said, 'I will confess my transgressions to the Lord'; / And You forgave the guilt of my sin" (Psalm 32:3, 5). Covering up sin, or excusing its presence, is a lamentable choice because it reveals that pride reigns. Pride causes us to run from facing our sin honestly. God commands us to humble ourselves (1 Peter 5:6), and that is our responsibility. James and Peter both refer to Proverbs 3:34, "GOD IS OPPOSED TO THE PROUD, BUT GIVES GRACE TO THE HUMBLE" (James 4:6, 1 Peter 5:5). Do you want God to oppose you or to give you grace? Every choice you make to be honest about your sinful failures cultivates humility. Jesus humbled Himself (Philippians 2:5–8). In order to follow Him, we must do the same. Jesus confronted our sin in death, and we must confront our sin by death to self with its horrendous pride. There is no other way if we will walk with God.

Conscience is the ethical sense organ of our beings. It is the inner faculty that distinguishes between morally right and morally wrong. *Conscience* is used thirty-two times in the New Testament. The Old Testament uses the word *heart* instead of *conscience*. The apostle Paul said, "I also do my best to maintain always a blameless conscience both before God and before men" (Acts 24:16). Paul writes in his first letter to Timothy (1:19) that some had "rejected [their good conscience] and suffered shipwreck in regard to their faith." 1 John 3:21–22 teaches that a stained conscience hinders confidence in prayer. In order to live in God's fullness, a clear conscience is imperative, both before God and before man.

How can your conscience be cleared? God's provision is twofold. First, the death of Christ was for every single sin of your entire life. The full price for all your sin has been paid. Jesus Christ's death fully satisfied God's justice. On heaven's side, nothing else needs to be done about your sins. Secondly, confession before Him is God's way for you to deal with your sins. The New Testament word for confession means, "to say the same thing." It means you say what God says about your sin. One by one by one, you name your sins before God calling them by their ugly names in full agreement with God about them. You understand that you have sinned against God who loves you and wants His very best for you. You then thank Him for His forgiveness and His cleansing from all unrighteousness. Again and again God's Word speaks of His forgiveness. Over and over He assures us that He freely forgives us when we come with godly sorrow and repentance because we have offended Him. 1 John 1:9 gives assurance, "If we confess our sins, He is faithful and righteous [just] to forgive us our sins and to cleanse us from all unrighteousness." Note that both forgiveness and cleansing are given when we confess.

Thanking Him for this magnificent gift of forgiveness and cleansing is very important. I once counseled a man who said that he had confessed a terrible sin over and over but could not find the peace of forgiveness. I said to him, "Have you thanked the Lord for His gift of forgiveness?" With a look of surprise he replied, "No." I suggested we get on our knees by my desk and that he thank God for His forgiveness. We did, and immediately peace came to his soul. When you receive a gift it is always proper to thank the giver.

A favorite verse of mine in the New Living Translation is Isaiah 44:22, "I have swept away your sins like the morning mists. I have scattered your offenses like the clouds. Oh, return to me, for I have paid the price to set you free." This fantastic assurance should fill our hearts with joy and gladness.

When we have sinned against another, we should go and ask for his or her forgiveness. Abandonment to Jesus means that we take this pathway of humility and of death to self with its dreadful pride. This is walking out abandonment to Jesus. Our pride will fiercely fight it. I recently said to my son, "Pride is a thousand-headed monster. You cut one head off and another quickly takes its place." If you have offended another by a wrong attitude, sinful words, a sinful deed, or selfish neglect, then you should go and clear your conscience with that individual. Say, "I was wrong. Will you forgive me?" Encourage him to speak forgiveness to you. If he will not, your conscience can still be clear. If he has also been wrong and asked for your forgiveness, speak your forgiveness to him.

When our daughter Laura was about twelve or thirteen years old, I corrected her very strongly for something she did to her brother that could cause him great fear. I then left to go speak in a series of meetings at a nearby church. While praying before the meeting, the Holy Spirit impressed me that I had corrected her as if she should have known better when in fact I had never taught her about the matter. I had sinned against her. I repented to the Lord in prayer and then called home to ask my daughter to forgive me. My wife answered the phone, and when I asked to speak to Laura, she said that she was taking a bath getting ready for bed. I told my wife what I had done and asked her to please tell Laura. I then could speak God's Word in the church service with a clear conscience. When I arrived home later that night, our daughter was already asleep. When I got ready for bed, I found a note on my pillow that said, "Daddy, I forgive you and I love you. Your daughter, Laura." This young girl ministered grace to her daddy.

Sometimes we sin against someone in the presence of others, or even against a group of people. When this happens we should make it right with all involved. This is done not only for the sake of our conscience before God and man, but also for the sake of our Christian witness to those people who saw us behave in a way unlike Jesus. God uses our humility to bless others.

If someone has sinned against you and does not ask for your forgiveness, what should you do? Fullness cannot exist in a heart closed to an offender. Others do offend and hurt us, and sometimes they are not even aware of it. We must carefully guard the attitudes of our hearts. Sinful attitudes can defile your soul and yet be covered up from others by a smile or pretended behavior. Jesus says, "Whenever you stand praying, forgive, if you have anything against anyone, so that your Father who is in heaven will also forgive you your transgressions" (Mark 11:25). Colossians 3:12–13 gives clear instruction, "So, as those who have been chosen of God, holy and beloved, put on a heart of compassion, kindness, humility, gentleness and patience; bearing with one another, and *forgiving each other, whoever has a complaint against anyone, just as the Lord forgave you, so also should you*" (italics added). Speak forgiveness for that person in prayer before the Lord. Otherwise the unresolved offense and hurt leads to anger, resentment, and eventually bitterness. Unforgiveness is sin and will hinder the Spirit's fullness. The only request in the model prayer Jesus gives commentary on is the necessity of forgiving others (Matthew 6:14–15). In Matthew 18:21–35, Jesus presses the point of how serious it is not to forgive another. He tells a parable and then says that the heavenly Father will hand those who harbor unforgiveness over to the torturers. What a grave consequence this is!

Ask the Lord to reveal anything to you that grieves Him—any attitudes, words, thoughts, habits, relationships, or omissions (things you should have done that you have not done). Sins you have already confessed are gone forever. If the devil accuses you of sins already confessed, remember and acknowledge with thanksgiving that you already have the Lord's forgiveness by the blood of Christ. Whatever sins the Lord may disclose to you, confess them one by one until your conscience is clear both before God and before man.

Then you will know the Holy Spirit is no longer grieved and you will have peace. When your life is cleansed and wholly available to the Lord, you then are a suitable temple for the Spirit to fill. You are still an unworthy vessel but not an unfit one.

Steadfast Trust for Fullness

As a young seminary student and then a pastor, as I told in the first chapter, I knew very little about the Holy Spirit. During my seminary training for the ministry I began to learn about men of recent history who had dramatic encounters with the Spirit that changed their lives and ministries. In my ignorance I thought I would have to have the same kind of dramatic encounter with the Holy Spirit that these well-known men had experienced. They had overwhelming feelings, so I must also. This would be a sign to me that I had found what I was searching for. I wanted some kind of spiritual experience that would assure me God's Spirit had come upon me as He had on these other men. I was ignorant of the difference between exceptional fillings by the Spirit for special ministry and a continual state of fullness for daily life and ministry. (Exceptional fillings by the Spirit will be explained in Chapter 7.) Also, I was not aware that some experience feelings when the Spirit fills them and others receive His fullness quietly by faith. Finally, I came to understand that just like salvation, fullness must be received by faith. A special feeling or experience is not necessary. What is essential, however, is that you prepare your heart for His fullness and then exercise faith to receive the promise of the Father.

As a sixteen year old, I had believed the gospel without any experience or feeling and thereby became a new person with new desires. So the fullness, like every other promise, must be received by faith. If I met God's conditions, I could trust Him to keep His promise. The issue was this: Would I believe Him? Would I trust Him to keep His Word? Would I fasten my heart to His promises and steadfastly trust for His answer? Someone has said that God is pleased when we hold His promises before Him. Another has said that His promises are like checks made out to us that we cash at the bank of heaven. Steadfast faith is the issue (James 1:6).

As a young pastor, I was learning about trusting God to keep His promises, and some lessons were hard. A pastor friend invited me to speak at a youth retreat of twenty high school seniors, plus the pastors and counselors. During this time I was learning about trusting God to keep His Word regarding the rivers He promised that would flow out. "Dear Father, You promised that if I believed, rivers would flow. I trust You for this. You also promised in Luke 11:13 that if I would ask for the Holy Spirit, You would give Him." I prayed holding on to His promises. I knew I desperately needed this if anything of eternal value was going to happen.

I arrived to discover a group of very worldly church youth. I was scheduled to deliver four messages from Friday night until Saturday night, at which time I had to return home for my Sunday morning responsibilities. I had an outstanding singer with me who would lead in some songs of praise and then sing a solo before I spoke. These youth had no interest in spiritual things. *None!* After I spoke, they got up, played their rock music tapes, and did their worldly things. I was heartsick. I took the two younger men I had brought with me to my bedroom, got down by my bed, and prayed. I remember putting my face on the bunk bed and crying out before God claiming His promises. I gave the second message. Immediately after I finished, they put on their music and began dancing. Back to my room I went with those two young men, got down, and wept before God pleading His promises. When the third message ended on Saturday afternoon nothing had changed. Saturday night before the last session, I was on my knees in my room crying out before God, "You have promised! You have promised! You have promised!" Until then there had been no indication at all of any change in the youth's attitudes or interest. They were very hard and resistant about spiritual matters. I then went into the meeting room to give my final message and spoke about the Lordship of Jesus Christ in a person's life. At the end of the message I said, "If Jesus Christ is the Lord of your life, I want you to stand up and confess out loud that He is the Lord of your life. If He is not and you want Him to be, then stand and say, "I want Jesus Christ to be the Lord of my life." After a long pause, one stood and confessed Christ's Lordship. Then slowly, one by one, others began to stand and say, "I want Jesus Christ to be my Lord." I cannot describe what happened in those moments. Suddenly Jesus was in our midst. The Holy Spirit came upon that group. Eighteen out of twenty young people bowed in submission to Christ's Lordship, plus the one who confessed His Lordship. One young lady would not yield to Christ and ran out of the room.

The pastor who had invited me called later in the week to tell me what had happened. These youth returned home on the bus reading their Bibles, praying, and singing all the way back home for the two and one-half hour trip. They gave testimonies in their church for the Sunday night service that lasted as long as their bus trip. They began Bible studies at school and went to other churches to give testimony of what had happened in their lives.

This was a very important lesson for me about the value of trusting God to keep specific promises in the face of opposing forces and seemingly impossible circumstances. What I experienced with those youth was a spiritual conflict that required pressing through in prayer by using God's promises as a weapon in battle. Trusting God for His fullness is a different matter. He wants to give you His fullness far more than you want to receive it. When you dispense with the issues in your life that may hinder Him from filling you, then you may drink freely by steadfastly trusting Christ to fill you with His Spirit.

Regardless of your feelings, or experiences, or fiery darts of doubt from the evil one, trust Him to keep His Word. *Do not look for an experience, and do not wait for a feeling.* Do not examine your life to see if it has happened, and do not expect some dramatic evidence. Focus on His faithfulness to keep His Word. And believe. He commands you to be continually filled; therefore you know that it is His will for you to be continually filled. "This is the confidence which we have before Him, that, if we ask anything according to His will, He hears us. And if we know that He hears us in whatever we ask, we know that we have the requests which we have asked from Him" (1 John 5:14–15). Make note of this: When we ask according to His will then we can know that we have it. In Mark 11:24, Jesus instructs us, "Therefore I say to you, all things for which you pray and ask, believe that you have received them, and they will be granted you." He said we should ask believing we have received them. In

Luke 11:13, Jesus promised, "If you then, being evil, know how to give good gifts to your children, how much more will your heavenly Father give the Holy Spirit to those who ask Him?" This is powerful assurance about our heavenly Father's promise to answer. "Ask" is in the present tense, meaning to "keep on asking." I continue asking for the fullness to this very day and trust my faithful heavenly Father to answer. God will reveal His fullness in you and through you in His own way and in His own time. He knows exactly how and when to encourage you.

Andrew Murray wisely wrote in the late eighteen hundreds how the fullness comes to different ones: "To some it comes as a glad and sensible quickening (something felt) of their spiritual life. They are so filled with the Spirit that all their feelings are stirred. They can speak of something they have distinctly experienced as a gift from the Father. To others it is given, not to their feelings, but to their faith. It comes as a deep, quiet, but clearer insight into the fullness of the Spirit in Christ as indeed being theirs, and a faith that feels confident that His sufficiency is equal to every emergency that may arise. In the midst of weakness they know that the Power is resting on them. In either case they know that the blessing has been given from Above, to be maintained under obedience and deep dependence on Him from whom it came."[7] I have seen this to be true through the years.

Thirst! Come! Drink! And rivers will flow out! Jesus clearly marked out the path for the blessing of His Spirit.

L. L. Legters wrote, "Your evidence that you are filled with the Spirit is that Jesus becomes everything to you. You see Him. You are occupied with Him. You are fully satisfied with Jesus. He becomes real, and when you witness about Him, the Holy Spirit witnesses with you regarding the truth about Him."[8]

Blessed Lord,

I am ashamed for the times I have not lived in Your fullness. I am profoundly grateful for Your forgiveness, free to me, but infinitely costly to You. I come asking that You work in me all of Your good pleasure so that I thirst for You more than anything else. I praise You that You have embraced me by Your astonishing and inexplicable love, and invite me to wholly entrust myself to that love. I am grateful the path to Your fullness is abundantly clear. Please, dear Lord, enable me to walk down this path into this abundant life You have promised and lavished upon me. I desire that Your life would flow through me so that others might be refreshed just as if You had passed by. I ask this for Your honor and glory. Lord, always and only for Your glory! Amen.

Notes

[1] Legters, *The Simplicity of the Spirit-filled Life*, 9.

[2] Lawrence O. Richards, *The Expository Dictionary of Bible Words*, (Grand Rapids, Michigan: Zondervan Publishing House, 1985), 348.

[3] J. Oswald Sanders, *Enjoying Intimacy with God*, (Grand Rapids, Michigan: Discovery House Publishers, 2000), 34.

[4] Ignatius of Antioch, Letter to the Romans, quoted by David Hazard, *You Give Me New Life*, (Minneapolis, Minnesota: Bethany House Publishers, 1995), 134–135.

[5] Oswald Chambers, *My Utmost for His Highest*, (Grand Rapids, Michigan: Discovery House Publishers, 1992), May 23.

[6] J. Wilbur Chapman, public domain excerpt from *Receive Ye the Holy Ghost?* dated 1881 and reprinted in *The Contemporaries Meet the Classics on the Holy Spirit*, compiled by Randall Harris, (West Monroe, LA: Howard Publishing Co., Inc. 2004), 146.

[7] Andrew Murray, *The Spirit of Christ*, (London, England: Oliphants LTD., 1963), 220–221.

[8] Legters, *The Simplicity of the Spirit-filled Life*, 51.

CHAPTER FIVE

The Way to Continue in Fullness

For many years now I have recited to myself every day the nine-fold fruit of the Spirit in Galatians 5:22–23, and have prayed for the fullness of the Spirit. For the chief mark of the fullness of the Spirit is the fruit of the Spirit: love, joy, peace, patience, kindness, good-ness, faithfulness, meekness, and self-control.
—John Stott, *Authentic Christianity*

A month before my dad was diagnosed with stomach cancer, my parents moved into a retirement home that is a lovely tri-level facility, consisting of independent living, assisted living, and personal (nursing) care. This would be their final home until they departed for their heavenly home. With this arrangement they each knew the other would be cared for when one passed away. The day came when Mom could no longer care for my dad in their apartment due to his weakened state and her arthritic back. She then made the difficult decision and had him moved to personal care where a trained nursing staff could take over and care for him. By this time Dad had accepted the fact that God was preparing to bring him home.

One morning I went downstairs alone to visit him. As we talked he said, "Son, I have the works for a nine-chime grandfather clock in my things in the woodworking shop. I was planning to build a cabinet for those works, but now I won't be able to." My dad had built other clocks and this was to be his final one, and the most expensive. He continued instructing me, "On the table by my chair in the apartment is a clock catalog. In it is a cherry cabinet that these works will fit into. I want you to order the cabinet and put it on my credit card. Would you put the works in the cabinet? I want to leave it as a legacy for my family." I told him I would, and later on I brought the catalog to him to make sure I had chosen the right cabinet. I then ordered it and delayed the shipping until I knew I would be home long enough to receive it.

After Dad went to heaven, the company sent the large, beautiful cherry clock cabinet to our house. Now I faced the challenge of putting the nine-chime works into the cabinet. Something I had never done before. As time permitted, and calling on the Lord to help me, I figured out how to put it together. Having accomplished the feat, I moved the clock hands to the hour to hear it chime. It played its lovely tune. I realized then that Dad, who wanted so much to build this clock, would never hear the tune nor hear it chime. I called Mom by phone and let her hear the chimes across the nine-hundred-plus miles. She listened and cried. The clock now sits in the entrance hallway of our home and every quarter hour makes its melodious sound, which continually reminds me of my dad's last priceless gift to me.

Three observations I make from this account. First, I gratefully received this expensive gift from my father. Secondly, I honored him by doing what he desired and asked of me. Thirdly, I now enjoy the beauty and purpose of his gracious gift. But a very important part of receiving and enjoying to the fullest his gift is to continue to maintain the clock's inner works in its proper operating condition by winding it regularly, keeping it clean, and keeping it lubricated.

In the same way the gift of the clock came from my earthly father to me, our heavenly Father has given to us a priceless gift in the Person of the Holy Spirit in all His fullness. With gratitude we should receive this priceless gift from our Father and honor Him by being obedient, and we should be thoroughly enjoying the beauty of His holy presence within us and maintain this gift through the providential means our Lord has appointed to each one of us. Fullness should be a continual state of being in our lives. If it is not, we will revert right back to trying to live in the strength of our own self-directed lives.

How do we continue in fullness? Jesus perfectly illustrated how in His teaching of John 15:1–11 with the picture of a vineyard. The vine is the sole source of the branch's life. The branch is useless and fruitless without the vine's life flowing into it (v. 4). Our heavenly Father is the Vinedresser who has one purpose for His vineyard—fruit, more fruit, and much fruit (vv. 1, 2, and 8). Continual fruitfulness requires continual pruning, so the Vinedresser keeps on cutting away old life so new growth occurs (v. 2). Keepers of vineyards tell us that only new growth bears new fruit. It is the Word Jesus speaks to us that cleanses away our old life (v. 3). Our part is to abide in Christ very simply by continually receiving His Word and by keeping His commandments so we abide in His love. Abiding in God's love, thirsting for and drinking of His life through His Word, and trusting Him regardless of what struggles we have leads to experiencing His own consummate joy and having our joy made full (v. 11). Herein is true satisfaction and fulfillment in daily living. This is life abundant (John 10:10).

Abiding in God's Love

Chapter 2 addresses the fundamental importance of enjoying a love relationship with the Lord. Like any relationship of love, this one must also be nurtured and cultivated. The original disciples were enamored with Jesus. They adored Him. He was the preeminent focus of their devotion and the incomparable passion of their souls. He occupied their minds, hearts, and affections above all else. He was real to them, not some distant personality who lived, died a horrific death, and was resurrected. They enjoyed His presence, and love for Him engulfed their souls. The apostle Paul uttered the passion of his heart when he wrote, "I want to know Christ," (Philippians 3:10 NIV) and "the love of Christ controls us" (2 Corinthians 5:14).

The love of God arrested their hearts. John wrote, "We have come to know and have believed the love which God has for us" (1 John 4:16). They treasured the love of God who cherished them, and their response was to love Him with abandon.

We also swim in the boundless ocean of His love. God wants us to relish His astounding grace, revel in His love, and cherish His compassion. He desires that we rest in His secure embrace and delight in the wonder of His tender care. He wants us to be wholly gratified with Him and enjoy His blazing love for us. God could not think of us with a more tender love than He does every nano-second. As His children, we are infinitely precious in His sight. We can go to bed conscious that we sleep in His love and awake the next morning remembering His personal, compassionate affection toward us. Psalm 48:9 in the New Living Translation reads, "O God, we meditate on your unfailing love as we worship in your Temple." The same translation says in another place, "For I am constantly aware of your unfailing love" (Psalm 26:3).

As you become more aware of God's love for you and gain a deeper understanding of that love, you will be able to love Him more and to love those around you, as well. "We love, because He first loved us" (1 John 4:19). In other words, God's love equips us to love Him and others (Ephesians 3:18–19, 4:1–3, 5:1–2). Paul wrote to the Thessalonians, "And may the Lord cause you to increase and abound in love for one another, and for all people, just as we also do for you" (1 Thessalonians 3:12). Not long afterwards, he wrote again in his second letter to them, "We ought always to give thanks to God for you, brethren, as is only fitting, because your faith is greatly enlarged, and the love of each one of you toward one another grows ever greater" (2 Thessalonians 1:3). Remembering Jesus' restful instruction teaching us how to abide in Him, He said, "Just as the Father has loved Me, I have also loved you; abide in my love" (John 15:9). "If you keep My commandments, you *will* abide in My love" (John 15:10, italics added). The clear implication is that to abide in His love produces rivers of His love flowing through us to others continuously (John 7:38). John further illumines this in his first letter, "This is His commandment, that we believe in the name of His Son Jesus Christ, and love one another, just as He commanded us" (1 John

3:23). The singular verb indicates that the two parts are tied together. To trust Christ is to love as He loves. God clearly enunciates that we are to know His love experientially, abide in His love faithfully, and grow constantly in our love—for Him and for others.

Sinful failure is traceable to failure to love. Peter failed his Master by denying that he even knew Him (Matthew 26:67–75), but the Lord confronted him about it down by the sea in a resurrection appearance, and asked, "Peter, do you love me?" (John 21:15–19). Jesus never asked Peter why he denied Him, but rather He went straight to the cardinal question, "Do you love Me?" This is the primary issue. With steadfast and tender love, Jesus reinstated Peter to full fellowship with Himself. He will also do the same for you when you fail.

The church at Ephesus must have been a healthy church because Paul did not offer any strong corrections in his letter to them written around AD 60. However, in Revelation 2:1–7 (written around AD 95) when the Lord spoke to the Ephesian church, He mentioned the commendable things about them—strong characteristics that we would look for in a very good and healthy church. Then He said, "But I have this against you, that you have left your first love" (Revelation 2:4). Another translation says, "You have abandoned the love you had at first" (ESV). These two scriptural illustrations disclose how central and consequential love for Christ is in our ongoing relationship with Him. Fasten your heart on a love relationship with Jesus. Cultivate it, and guard your heart diligently (Proverbs 4:23). As we grow in our love for Him so we grow in our obedience to Him.

Oswald Chambers wrote in his diary on August 20, 1908, "The great hunger is on me more than ever for Him and His work. O how few love Him and how feeble is my passionate love. I scarcely know anyone who is consumed for Him. It is all for creeds and phrases and belief, but for Him how few! To know Him—that is it."[1]

Ever Thirsting, Ever Drinking

How do you nurture a growing love relationship with Jesus? Quite simply, it is nourished when you spend time alone with Him. Staying on the path of fullness requires staying in close communion with your Lord. James wrote, "Draw near to God and He will draw near to you" (James 4:8). Here is an exquisite promise! Can you imagine anything more magnificent than Almighty God personally drawing near to you? Your heavenly Father cherishes your nearness. He delights when you share your heart with Him and when you hear His heart. Here is intimacy beyond anything the world can offer, and it is more personal than any other relationship you can have. It is exhilarating, satisfying, stimulating, and peaceful. This is drinking from heaven's abundant living water that flows from the throne of God (Psalm 36:8). God's plan is for you to be near Him for continuous fellowship, to continue drinking of His life through meditation on His Word (Psalm 1:1–3), to know Him ever more deeply (Philippians 3:10), to become like Him in heart and soul, and to become a living expression of His beautiful character as rivers of His love flow from you to those around you.

Julian of Norwich (1342–1413) told so well about God's nearness when she wrote, "Yes, it is true our Lord dwells with us now. He is in us, here present, embracing us and enclosing us in himself, never to leave us, nearer than we can say in failing human words . . . He who is all your joy is near to you right now—in this moment. He could not be closer if He were holding you, pressing you to himself, your two faces touching. It is the embrace of the Spirit, as the Beloved draws you into himself."[2]

Disciplining Your Life

Neglecting time alone with your Lord will impoverish you. You will be drawn away by your own selfish desires, the attraction of the world, and the ruthless attack of the enemy. One cannot continue in fullness if he or she does not continue drinking of His life, and this requires self-discipline. Thirst must find expression through self-discipline because discipline is necessary for godliness (1 Timothy 4:7). Sometimes Christians confuse discipline with legalism. The Olympic athlete with his eye on a gold medal is not *legalistic* because he disciplines himself for the purpose of winning, but rather he is *self-disciplined* because he wants to win. Longing to be the best motivates him to prepare for the competition, and that is not always easy. If you have your heart set on the goal of knowing and seeing

God and becoming like Jesus, then discipline is necessary in order to fulfill your desire. You will have to make choices against an enemy whose intent is to rob you of a close and affectionate relationship with Jesus. The devil will even use good things to hinder you. Jesus let nothing, even ministry to the masses and the needs of suffering humanity and lost people dying and going to hell, keep Him from necessary time alone with His heavenly Father (Luke 5:15–16).

Dallas Willard said it well: "When Jesus walked among humankind there was a certain simplicity to being his disciple. Primarily it meant to go with him, in an attitude of study, obedience, and imitation . . . We cannot literally be with him in the same way as his first disciples could. But the priorities and intentions—the heart and inner attitudes—of disciples are forever the same. In the heart of a disciple there is a desire, and there is decision or settled intent. Having come to some understanding of what it means, and thus having 'counted up the costs,' the disciple of Christ desires above all else to be like him."[3]

Donald Whitney wrote, "This daily devotion habit is not easy to develop because we lead busy lives and have an Enemy aware of the stakes involved. Missionary martyr Jim Elliot knew the battle: 'I think the devil has made it his business to monopolize on three elements: noise, hurry, crowds . . . Satan is quite aware of the power of silence.'"[4]

The last fruit of the Spirit listed is self-control (Galatians 5:23). By the Spirit empowering you through His fullness you can exercise self-control to make the necessary choices to be alone with your Lord—in quietness, without hurry, and away from people. With scarred hands outstretched Jesus says, "Come to Me" (Matthew 11:28). "Learn from Me, for I am gentle and humble in heart (Matthew 11:29). "Abide in Me" (John 15:4). By inference He said, "Love me" (John 14:15, 23). It is about relationship with Him as a Person—extremely personal and incredibly intimate. It is about becoming focused on His honor and His heart. Your greatest pleasure will come from delighting Him. Oswald Chambers wrote in his journal July 12, 1909, "How few of us are concerned about satisfying His heart. How I hear Him saying, 'I thirst, give me to drink.' May my Lord never let me grow cold in my longing to be a cup in His hand for the quenching of His own royal thirst."[5]

Gazing upon His Beauty

When I was a fourteen-year-old boy, two years before I became a Christian, I attended my first summer Baptist youth conference. I went because my friends were going and it sounded like fun. There was a guest speaker for the week who brought a message each evening to the hundreds of youth and their adult counselors. During the morning we met in small classes on various subjects, and at night we all met together in a large wooden structure used like an auditorium for a worship service. I do not remember anything else that was said during the week, but I remember well one thing said in an evening service. The guest pastor kept repeating these two lines throughout his sermon:

> Every morning lean thine arms awhile upon the windowsill of heaven and gaze upon the Lord. Then with a vision in thine heart, turn strong to meet the day. —Author unknown

Even though I was not a Christian at the time, it is like these words were carved into my memory. Apart from my awareness the Lord must have planted them deep within my heart that summer night so long ago and kept them securely there to direct my steps over these many years.

Thirsting and being alone with Jesus should lead to gazing on His beauty. As surely as we can gaze upon a beautiful sunset with our physical eyes, so we can gaze upon our holy God with our inner eyes. Jesus spoke about the pure of heart seeing God (Matthew 5:8). Paul wrote about gazing upon the glory of God and being transformed by what we see into that same image (2 Corinthians 3:18). John wrote about the return of Christ, "We know that when He appears, we will be like Him, because we will see Him just as He is" (1 John 3:2). Is that not an extraordinary thought? So resplendent and powerful is a sustained view of Jesus that it transfigures us to become like Him. In His prayer to God the Father recorded in John 17, Jesus prayed for our ultimate experience in heaven, which is to see His glory that the Father has given Him (John 17:24). On earth we catch glimpses of His glory through His Word made alive to us, through the Holy Spirit's revelation of Christ's presence to us, and through what we see Him do by His power—and we long for more. We anticipate heaven where we will have an unhindered and uninterrupted view of Him in all of His pure, holy brilliance.

To see the Lord's beauty with the eyes of your heart is to increasingly love Him. To catch glimpses of Him now, however dim those glimpses may be, fills our hearts with wonder, awe, admiration, and reverence. His loveliness humbles us, and draws from us a desire to love Him more and a craving to know Him more intimately. It is like finding a gold nugget in an old mine; once you find one, you want to search until you find another. Spurgeon wrote, "We would rather have one mouthful of Christ's love, and a sip of his fellowship, than a whole world full of carnal delights."[6]

How do you gaze upon God? What does it mean to see Him with the eyes of your own heart? It means to contemplate His character, to mentally look upon His personhood reflecting upon various aspects of His character. It means to *meditate* upon the truth about Him revealed in Scripture. Dr. J. I. Packer wrote the best definition of meditation I have ever read:

> How can we turn our knowledge *about* God into knowledge *of* God? The rule for doing this is demanding, but simple. It is that we turn each truth that we learn *about* God into matter for meditation *before* God, leading to prayer and praise *to* God . . .
>
> Meditation is the activity of calling to mind, and thinking over, and dwelling on, and applying to oneself, the various things that one knows about the works and ways and purposes and promises of God. It is an activity of holy thought, consciously performed in the presence of God, under the eye of God, by the help of God, as a means of communion with God. Its purpose is to clear one's mental and spiritual vision of God, and to let His truth make its full and proper impact on one's mind and heart.[7]

Julian of Norwich wrote, "God tells us in His Word to fix our minds on what is high and holy and pure. (See Philippians 4:8–9.) We do this in contemplation. He wants us to practice contemplation as often as possible, for as long as we can, as His grace gives us strength. I am referring to silent prayer in which we fix our soul on the invisible attributes of God—His goodness, love and the like. This prayer fills us with the peace that comes from God, a serenity that is like experiencing the glory of heaven itself, while it lasts."[8]

Kris Lundgaard, an author of two excellent books strongly endorsed by Christian leaders, points out the difficulty with the discipline of our minds for contemplation:

> Our minds are accustomed to other entertainment and aren't in shape for the faith-work of reflecting on Christ. That may be why most of us live at low spiritual tide, powerless and joyless in our religion.
>
> But if we were in love with Christ, so that we couldn't wait to see him again—and if we were in the spiritual habit of gazing on him and marveling at him—then our lives before God would be sweeter to us. Day by day our spirits would grow stronger. We would more carefully represent Christ to the world. Strange as it sounds, death would begin to sound inviting to us, as the final release from everything that distracts us from the sight of our Lord.
>
> *We have to prize seeing the glory of God in the face of Christ as the greatest privilege in this life.*[9]

Although you need to understand God's truth accurately, Bible knowledge alone will not transform you to be like Christ. Preaching, Bible study classes, worship services, and praise songs will not transfigure you, even though these are important for growth and church life. All these necessary components must be united with personally gazing upon Christ, enjoying His presence, and worshiping Him. Keith Price, who was mentored by A. W. Tozer, wrote, "Tozer often expressed his disgust at the common disease of substituting 'the grasping of the concept' for 'experiencing of the reality.'"[10]

Thirsting for Christ and gazing on Him causes us to keep on thirsting for His fullness. Experience teaches us the vital lesson that we cannot represent Him if we are not filled by Him. Just as John Stott indicated in the epigraph, we should day by day ask God to fill us with His Holy Spirit, and implicitly trust that He does.

Sometimes Struggling, Always Trusting

Abiding in the Father's love and living in the Spirit's fullness does not insulate us from difficult and painful experiences in life. Trials, testing, and temptations will be our lot. Jesus said, "In the world you have tribulation" (John 16:33). Jesus promised never to leave us (John 14:16, Matthew 28:20), but never did He promise life without painful trials. These come in many forms. There are seasons in life when we struggle more than usual with indwelling sin, and the conflict between flesh and Spirit becomes intense (Galatians 5:17). (We will consider this in the next chapter.) At other times we come under the Lord's hand of discipline so that we may share His holiness (Hebrews 12:10). There will be difficult relationships and hard circumstances we must walk through, but all of it is under the direct supervision of our loving heavenly Father and is for our eternal benefit. Occasionally you will receive painful news that suddenly turns your journey into dark days and sleepless nights. In short, life is hard, but all of it is within the sphere of God's goodness because we stand steadfastly in grace (Romans 5:2–5). Whatever comes our way presents an opportunity to learn more about God's steadfast love and absolute faithfulness. "All the paths of the Lord are steadfast love and faithfulness, for those who keep his covenant and his testimonies" (Psalm 25:10 ESV).

Because of a very difficult marriage, our daughter Laura had been separated from her husband for fifteen months. She was living in Boca Raton, Florida during which time the younger of her two sons, Jonathan, age four, developed a bronchial problem. When it persisted without responding to antibiotic treatment, she took him to have a routine X-ray. When the medical personnel came to give their report to her, she immediately knew it was serious. They had discovered a massive tumor in our grandson Jonathan's chest. It was pressing so heavily on his trachea it was life threatening. He had to be taken immediately to Miami Children's Hospital in Miami, Florida, and a doctor would accompany him in the ambulance for the hour and a half trip. Laura could not ride with them in the ambulance, but rather had to follow in her car. She asked them, "How will I know if he dies on the way?" They replied, "We will pull off onto the side of the road." "And then I can get in the ambulance to be with him?" she asked. They said, "Yes."

The anxious journey began. As Laura followed in her car, this Scripture came to her mind, "Do not fear, for I am with you; do not anxiously look about, for I am your God. I will strengthen you, surely I will help you, surely I will uphold you with My righteous hand" (Isaiah 41:10). She knew the Holy Spirit had given it to her because the Word promises, "But the Helper, the Holy Spirit, whom the Father will send in my name, He will teach you all things, and bring to your remembrance all that I said to you" (John 14:26). Over and over again she quoted the verse from Isaiah out loud as she drove.

Some months earlier while struggling with the disappointing circumstances of her marriage and its aftermath, she knelt down before the Lord and said, "Whatever you want, Lord, I will do it." And now while she drove, she once again acknowledged that she wanted the Lord's will to be done with Jonathan, whatever His will should be.

At the hospital, tests revealed that Jonathan had a very serious type of cancerous tumor. Thus began an eighteen-month journey of sleepless nights, long days of tender care for a sick child, little appetite for eating, days of waiting for the next doctors' report from many tests, and praying and hoping for the best—humanly speaking—but trusting for the Lord's best—eternally speaking.

Soon after receiving the X-ray results, Laura called us in Louisiana with the shocking news. Within a few hours we were on a plane to Miami arriving about midnight to be with her. Our hearts were indeed heavy with sorrow as we felt Laura's pain—her struggle with being alone and separated from her husband—and now this coming on top of it. Job, who suffered far more than we, asked, "Shall we indeed accept good from God and not accept adversity?" (Job 2:10). The Psalmist wrote, "I know, O LORD, that Your judgments are righteous, / And that in faithfulness You have afflicted me" (Psalm 119:75). The Lord alone could be our refuge (Psalm 46:1–3), and we would trust Him to be glorified no matter the outcome (Psalm 50:14–15). I discovered that the darker the night, the brighter the stars of God's truth shine. Isaiah 55:9 became especially comforting to me, "For as the heavens are higher than the earth, / So are My ways than your ways / And My thoughts than your thoughts." It was impossible for us to understand what God was doing. But we knew that in His love Jonathan's illness had eternal value for us all.

Laura made the decision that she would praise and worship the Lord through all that was to come, and she did. I was humbled and amazed by the flood of sustaining grace God gave to her. Naturally, throughout those eighteen months, there were times of anger, fear, and all the myriad emotions anyone experiences in such times, but always she was sustained and looked to the Lord and worshiped Him.

When the chemo treatments failed to stop the cancer, the doctors transferred Jonathan to a hospital in Columbia, South Carolina for a bone-marrow transplant. In Columbia Laura found a church with a strong Bible-teaching ministry, because she knew her need to be under the sound teaching of God's Word, and began attending. She attended worship services and Bible studies whenever possible. During the day when she could leave Jonathan, she would go for hour-long walks singing choruses and hymns of praise out loud to God. On one of our visits I saw a paper taped onto her bathroom mirror with these words written by George Herbert:

PRAISE

Praise!
      Praise!
            Praise!
Lord,
I will mean and speak
      Thy praise alone.
My busy heart shall
      spin it all my days,
and
      when it stops

for want of store,
then will I
wring it
with a sigh
or groan
that Thou may yet have more.[11]

Psalm 92:1 reminds us, "It is good to give thanks to the LORD, / And to sing praises to Your name, O Most High."

Again and again when Laura could not get to a Bible each day because of the demands of caring for Jonathan, the Holy Spirit would bring to her mind God's Word that she had stored in her heart, the specific Scriptures needed just for that very moment. In the midst of the pressure of those demanding days and nights, and the weariness of those months while in the crucible of heartache, questions and concerns would come to her mind. "Suppose I am not here when Jonathan dies because I got thirsty and went to get something to drink, or because I went to a Wednesday night Bible study?" These questions taunted her. Then one day one of her pastors from First Presbyterian Church, Mark Ross, who had been so helpful and encouraging to her, came by the hospital. They were standing outside Jonathan's room, and Laura expressed some of her concerns to him. Pastor Ross then reminded her of God's wonderful sovereignty and specific guidance for His children. He said, "Laura, when we are in the presence of Jesus we will realize we never had anything to worry about at all." These words were imprinted in her mind and immediately brought peace to her heart. She vividly remembers them to this day.

The day finally came when it was apparent Jonathan would soon go to be with Jesus. By now he was five years old and had trusted Jesus to be his Savior. Laura prepared him for his new home by telling him all about heaven. It was a Friday night. Many of those who had become dear and supportive friends of both Laura and Jonathan gathered in the hospital room, along with our families. Laura was sitting on the hospital bed holding her dying, precious son close to her and holding the blue oxygen tube near his nose attempting to make him as comfortable as possible. Jonathan's lungs were shutting down because of damage from the chemo treatments.

We watched the oxygen saturation monitor and knew it would not be long. In the room we—twelve or thirteen of us—sang choruses and hymns throughout the night while Laura assured Jonathan about heaven. He asked her if she would come. She told him she would. He asked when. She replied, "Soon." He was conscious to the very end, struggling to breathe, and it became more laborious for him as his lungs gradually shut down. Saturday morning about 5:23 AM while we were singing the Lord's Prayer, Jonathan went from the presence of our singing into the presence of the angels' singing. Our dear Jonathan went from his mother's arms of embrace into the arms of Jesus' embrace. The battle was finally over and the victory was won. There was a collective sigh of relief, and then stillness. After several moments of silence, Laura, still holding the warm but spiritually vacant body of her five-year-old dearest Jonathan, began to sing the chorus:

> God, You're so good!
> God, You're so good!
> God, You're so good,
> You're so good to me!

We all joined in once again singing and praising our wonderful and gracious and merciful God who Himself had given up His one and only Son so that we could know Him and have the secure knowledge of eternal life in heaven with Him for Jonathan, Laura, and the rest of us standing there.

After Jonathan died, Laura gave him a final bath in the hospital. She then went home to prepare her little boy's funeral service. She wanted it to be a time of worship with much singing to the glory of God.

The casket rolled down the aisle of the sanctuary of the large, historic First Presbyterian Church in Columbia, South Carolina. Walking in front of the casket as it moved slowly down the aisle was Pastor Ross, and walking behind the casket alone was our dear daughter Laura. As her parents we followed. She looked lovely with her blond hair, her pink suit a friend bought her for this occasion, and her radiant face. She looked so small because of the weight she had lost during the previous eighteen months, but Laura stood between her mother and me while singing praise and worshiping God with all her heart.

The hymn by Annie Johnson Flint is indeed true:

> He giveth more grace when the burden grows greater;
> He sendeth more strength when the labors increase.
> To added affliction He addeth His mercy;
> To multiplied trials, His multiplied peace. [12]

Grief does not go away when life turns a new direction, but continues as an unwanted companion. During Jonathan's sickness Laura had been divorced from her husband. In the singles group that surrounded and supported Laura during those Columbia days was a godly man, Randall A. Smith. He was a doctoral student at the University of South Carolina. Some months after Jonathan's death, Randy called to ask my permission to marry Laura. Their pastors, who had taught, discipled, and mentored them, and to whom they had made themselves accountable, agreed that biblically it was permissible and encouraged them to marry. By this time Randy knew he loved Laura and Benjamin, her firstborn, very much. They married and Randy took a position as professor of English and Creative Writing in a Christian college in Nyack, New York.

I understand that the death of a child is the most painful loss and grief that one can experience. Laura would go through seasons of agonizing grief. Never again this side of heaven would she be able to hear Jonathan's raspy voice, or run her fingers through his straight blond hair, or enjoy his energetic playfulness, or see his beautiful, round-faced smile. The hole left by Jonathan's absence would always be there; sometimes it was overwhelmingly and excruciatingly conspicuous. For months afterward when she was figuring the number of dishes she needed for supper, she would often count one setting too many, and suddenly realize with deep, stabbing pain that Jonathan was no longer there.

On the first anniversary of Jonathan's death Laura wrote us the following letter:

March 18, 1997

Before this time in my life whenever I heard the term "wail" I thought of it more as a description of an inward aching. I didn't imagine that people actually wailed out loud, but the term was used to describe what they felt like doing because of the pain that they felt on the inside. I have unwantingly come to know that a wail is indeed an out-loud lamentation that crescendos forth from our very viscera. It erupts from a grief that defies dignity, and any appropriateness of time or place. Often it feels that the only thing that will ever quiet me is to feel the warm weight of Jonathan in my lap with my cheek resting against his soft hair.

Off and on I have been needled by the enemy to believe that Jonathan's death was punishment for me. I think that in these last weeks that accusation has finally been silenced. As I walked in the cold air yesterday I examined what had been accomplished through his death. There are two things that I know. One is that God took my child who was more precious to me than my own life and transported him to a place where he will never know pain or sin or sickness. Jonathan lives in the presence of God's only Son and has been spared all the heartaches of this earth. And secondly, through all that has happened, God has revealed a portion of Himself to me—given a part of Himself to me—that I never knew was possible. I have known His love, His peace, and His presence in a way that has changed me forever. I know that He alone is reason enough to live and nothing that I long for compares to knowing Him.

I still have many unanswered questions. Days when my heart cries out, "Why? Why? Why?" I struggled angrily with the passage in Luke where Jesus has compassion on the widow whose son dies.

Jesus touches the coffin and brings the young man back to life. The Scripture then says that "Jesus gave him back to his mother." Why did God have compassion on her that he had not shown to me? After many months I finally realized that God had indeed shown me the same compassion. He had sacrificed His only Son to pay for sin, and in so doing had forever loosed the stranglehold of death. He would one day give me back my son and we would be together for eternity. And the result in me was the same result that occurred in the people who were with Jesus that day—I was "filled with awe and praised God." I said along with them, "God has come to help His people." What a loving and almighty God we have, who can come now to comfort us in the midst of death because He came before and conquered death in the midst of us.

Late last Saturday night as Randy and I lay in bed to go to sleep I began to cry. Randy felt my trembling and came close and wrapped his arms around me. And slowly my crying turned to wailing—loud laments for Jonathan. And as I cried in the darkness, Randy whispered aloud prayers to our heavenly Father on my behalf. I could not pray. I could barely nod my head in agreement with his prayers because my sobs so convulsed my body. At times I would grow quiet and he would pause, and then as he would pray again, I would cry out again. And this is how we lay for a long time.

I must tell you, that in me and through me and all around me, stronger than the pulsing ache for Jonathan, louder than my own crying out of his name, and deeper than the deepest visceral pain, was the reverberating, life-capturing truth of the utter goodness of my God.

With much love and gratefulness—
Your daughter, Laura

When I called Laura to ask for permission to tell this part of her story, we had a precious time of sharing eternal things. After I read to her what you have just read, she exclaimed, "God was so faithful!" Then she said, "Many Christians lose sight of the fact that God's interests are for eternity, and God's purpose here is for redemption and sanctification. God's purpose is not to make us happy. We live in the now. God lives in the eternal. We need to have eternity in view now. God wants to conform us now into the likeness of Christ."

Standing in Laura's kitchen window is a large, antique letter "E" painted with bright red enamel. It is there to remind her every morning when she comes down from their upstairs bedroom that she must live today with eternity in view. She does not want to lose that perspective in the midst of her busy demands and the distractions of daily life. She says, "I want to remember how we should live. After ten years it is so easy to forget."

Summary

The filling of God's Spirit is not a one-time experience, but rather an ongoing relationship. This fullness flows from a love relationship with Jesus. It is maintained by keeping a clean conscience, continuing wholly yielded to Him as Lord, drinking regularly from the Fountain of His Life by intimate and personal communion with Him through prayer and meditation in His Word, and asking for His fullness. The longer you walk this way the greater your desire and capacity for His fullness becomes within you. Then the more His lovely character becomes visible through your unique personality. Not only does this fullness in your life glorify God, it also deeply satisfies your own heart.

Any Christian life not filled with the Holy Spirit is like a rosebud that never blooms, wheat that never becomes bread, and fruit that never ripens in sweetness. It is indeed a rosebud and wheat and fruit, but never does it fulfill its destiny for the pleasure of God and the enjoyment and growth of others.

The question before us now is this: What does it mean to walk by the Spirit? Read on.

Holy Loving Father,

With love higher than the highest heavens You have blessed me. I cannot begin to grasp the length, and breadth, and depth, and height of Your love for me. You have given me Yourself to be who You are in me and through me to others. So often who I am is seen instead of who You are. What I really want is for the fragrance of Your love to be upon me like a rose in full bloom. I am willing for my self-life to be ground like wheat so I can become the bread of life in my Lord's hands. I long to be sweetened like fully ripened fruit so the sweetness of Christ's character flows from my inner being out to others. I want the quality of my life to be unexplainable.

Blessed Lord, there is no other way but by Your Holy Presence in all Your fullness in my life. With cleansed hands, a purified heart, and a wholly yielded life, I ask for You to fill me with Your Holy Spirit. And keep on filling me until I am with You in heaven. Through Jesus my Lord and for Your glory I ask it. Amen!

Notes

[1] David McCasland, *Oswald Chambers: Abandoned to God*, (Grand Rapids, Michigan: Discovery House Publishers, 1993), 142.

[2] Julian of Norwich, *I Promise You a Crown*, Devotional Readings arranged and paraphrased by David Hazard, (Minneapolis, Minnesota: Bethany House Publishers, 1995), 149–150.

[3] Dallas Willard, *The Spirit of the Disciplines*, (San Francisco: HarperCollins Publishers, 1988), 260–261.

[4] Donald Whitney, *Spiritual Disciplines for the Christian Life*, (Colorado Springs, Colorado: NavPress, 1992), 187.

[5] McCasland, *Oswald Chambers: Abandoned to God*, 167.

[6] C. H. Spurgeon, *Morning & Evening*, (Scotland, Great Britain: Christian Focus Publications, 1994), January 8, Evening reading.

[7] J. I. Packer, *Knowing God*, (Downers Grove, Illinois: InterVarsity Press, 1973), 18–19.

[8] Norwich, *I Promise You a Crown*, 127–128.

[9] Kris Lundgaard, *Through the Looking Glass*, (Phillipsburg, New Jersey: P & R Publishing, 2000), 27.

[10] Keith Price, *Thirsting After God*, (Camp Hill, Pennsylvania: Christian Publications, 2000), 261.

[11] George Herbert, "Praise," Unable to document original source.

[12] Annie Johnson Flint, "He Giveth More Grace."

CHAPTER SIX

In Step with the Spirit

They passed through the Phrygian and Galatian
region, having been forbidden by the Holy Spirit to
speak the word in Asia; and after
they came to Mysia, they were trying
to go into Bithynia,
and the Spirit of Jesus did not permit them.
—Acts 16:6–7

Since we live by the Spirit,
let us keep in step with the Spirit.
—Galatians 5:25 (NIV)

The New International Version used above translates Galatians 5:25 accurately. The usual Greek word used for "walk" means how you conduct yourself, referring to your daily behavior. In Galatians 5:25, however, the word for walk is a different word. It is "an exhortation to keep in step with one another in submission of heart to the Holy Spirit, and therefore of keeping step with Christ."[1] Dr. J. I. Packer, the respected theologian and scholar, says this word "carries the thought of walking in line, holding to a rule, and thus proceeding under another's control."[2]

When I was in high school I played in my Dad's band. Autumn was our marching season and spring was our concert season. In late summer and through autumn, we practiced marching. This was during football season when we had to prepare new music and a half-time marching show each week to present at Friday night football games. We would also march in various parades, and participate in a well-known band festival contest where we competed before a panel of highly qualified judges. It was very important that we know how to march in a straight line, keep in step with one another, and maintain the correct distance between each of the rows. Each new school year we began by marching on the road around the stadium to a drum-beat. We drilled and drilled until it was like second nature to stay in step with the cadence of the drums, maintain straight lines, and retain the proper distance between rows. Having practiced marching sufficiently, we then added the instruments and the musical arrangements to make the sound our director wanted. If someone got out of step, there was a stutter-step that would put that person back in step with the others. It was crucial to be able to hear the drumbeat or the beat of the music to stay in step. We had a drum major who led the band when we marched, and we followed his direction. Of course, we wanted to please our director, who had high standards, as well as perform to the best of our ability.

In the same way, keeping in step with the Spirit requires that we be able to know God's will, His direction through His Word, to hear His quiet, gentle impressions, and to maintain a willingness to go wherever He leads and do whatever He desires. Daily we are enveloped with our worldly concerns. But toleration of any known sin and the reign of self-will will drown out the voice of the Spirit and prevent us from hearing Him and doing His will. We are then out of step with the Spirit, and the flesh rules. (Flesh is our human nature ruled by sin and self.) It becomes difficult to choose against the flesh because the Spirit is squelched. Two sad results occur: We lose the joy and peace that come from the Spirit's fullness, and we dishonor Jesus with our behavior. Both results grieve the Spirit.

A Continuing Conflict

Choosing against sin and temptation is a constant battle for Spirit-filled believers. Fullness in the Spirit does not end the conflict. Fleshly desires are still resident within us and crave to rule over our lives (Romans 6:12, Galatians 5:17). The power of sin is always present within us and relentlessly pursues us to reign over us, even in our holiest moments. Indwelling sin unremittingly opposes the Spirit who lives in us and struggles for mastery over us. The only answer is to walk by the Spirit. It is important to remember: There is no other answer to this dilemma because God says, "But I say, walk by the Spirit, and you will not carry out the desire of the flesh" (Galatians 5:16). We either walk by the Spirit or we carry out the desires of our flesh. The choice is ours.

J. Oswald Sanders uses an excellent illustration:

> As we walk by the Spirit, following His promptings, the voice of fleshly desire will lose its power to allure. In his book *White Fang*, Jack London told of an animal of that name who was half-wolf, half-dog. One day White Fang strayed into a hen-run and killed several hens. The owner was naturally very angry. White Fang's trainer said to him, "I will guarantee that he will remain a whole afternoon in the hen-run and not kill a single chicken."
>
> The test began. Whenever the old lust to kill asserted itself, his master's voice recalled White Fang again and again, until at last the force of the impulse had spent itself as he listened to that quietly restraining voice. He finally fell asleep in the midst of the hens. When he woke up, he yawned and jumped out of the hen-run. The temptation had no more power to allure. White Fang's victory over his wolf-nature sprang from the restraining power of his loved master's voice. So with us. Sensitive obedience to the restraining and empowering voice of the Spirit brings victory.

That is not the mere damming back of the temptation, only for it to break out once again, worse than ever. It is the counteracting operation of a higher and more powerful law (Romans 8:2).[3]

Hindering the Spirit

Scripture commands, "Do not quench the Spirit" (1 Thessalonians 5:19). "Do not quench" means "do not put out the Spirit's fire." If you lick your fingers and put them over a burning candlewick to extinguish it, you have quenched its fire. No longer can it burn. If you resist the Spirit's promptings, direction, and empowering, He is quenched. His will is denied, and no longer can He have His way. He is prevented from performing the Father's will through your life. He will not force you, but rather He awaits your full submission and cooperation. This is God's way of love and respect for us as persons, allowing us to choose.

In Christ Christians are set free from living by an external code of conduct, which is the Law (Galatians 5:1). Christ fulfilled the Law for us (Romans 10:4). Life in the Spirit is by relationship with Him. Relationship cannot be reduced to a formula of rules and regulations; to do so destroys any meaningful intercourse between two persons. Furthermore, rules and regulations ruin the enjoyment of it. Relationship lives and grows by intimate communion between two persons. Keeping in step with the Spirit is walking in communion with a Person. The Holy Spirit is Jesus in you and with you here and now. To obey the Spirit is to follow Christ. A relationship of love gives freedom and spontaneous expression—sometimes extravagant expression—of love between you and Him. This is the necessary motive for staying in step with the Spirit. Jesus said, "If you love Me, you will keep my commandments" (John 14:15). As stated in an earlier chapter, the accent falls on loving Him in the most intimate of relationships. Obedience then follows.

Acts 16:6–7 (quoted in the epigraph) indicates that the Spirit both directs and prevents the steps of His servants. His role, as Counselor, is to teach, counsel, and lead in the fulfilling of God's will so that Jesus is glorified because His will is done. If the Spirit directed the Apostle Paul to fulfill God's will and plan, then He will direct you to fulfill His will and plan. Herein you will find your greatest joy. The alternative is futility, emptiness, and frustration within your Christian life.

Love for Jesus is expressed by absolute submission to Him and total dependence upon Him. This, of course, is to the measure of your understanding and limit of your maturity at any given point in your development. Increasingly, you will learn more about what absolute submission and total dependence requires of you as you mature spiritually. As you continue in step with the Spirit, you will mature and your capacity for His fullness will increase for Christ's greater honor—thirtyfold, sixtyfold, and even a hundredfold.

Three guiding principles will help you to learn how to stay in step with the Spirit: obeying God's Word, doing the next thing, and following His inner promptings.

Knowing and Obeying God's Word

Understanding and obeying God's Word is requisite for keeping in step with His Spirit. "All Scripture is inspired by God and profitable for teaching, for reproof, for correction, for training in righteousness" (2 Timothy 3:16). The primary way we know God's will is by knowing what God has said in His inspired Word, and also by knowing how to apply it practically in our daily lives. In Colossians 1:9 Paul wrote, "For this reason also, since the day we heard of it, [their salvation] we have not ceased to pray for you and to ask that you may be filled with the knowledge of His will in all spiritual wisdom and understanding." Paul's first burden for these recent converts, who were probably his spiritual grandchildren, was that they be filled with the knowledge of God's will. Knowledge of God's Word is required for those who will live the will of God. Knowledge of God's will includes two parts: wisdom and understanding. The word "spiritual" means it comes by the Holy Spirit. He must reveal spiritual truth to the human heart, and He alone can do it. It is impossible for us to know it in our hearts without the Spirit teaching us. We may understand with our minds the words, concepts, and principles from reading the Bible or from human teachers, but only the Spirit of Christ can reveal the truth deep inside and apply it to our hearts. We are wholly dependent on Him for this inner enlightenment. Paul prayed similarly for the Ephesians when he prayed, "That the God of our Lord Jesus Christ, the Father of glory, may give to you a spirit of wisdom and of revelation in the knowledge of Him. I pray that the eyes of your heart may be enlightened" (Ephesians 1:17–18). We should pray this for ourselves and for others. Truly, God gives as we ask, and ask we must.

Also, the Spirit alone can give us wisdom. Wisdom is the ability to know how to apply practically the knowledge the Spirit reveals. For example, the Word commands us to love with God's love. Love is just a word, but by the Spirit love becomes revelation and reality. When the Spirit reveals this Divine love to our hearts, and then shows us how to express this love specifically in everyday relationships, the Word is made flesh through us. The Spirit's fullness bears the fruit of God's love through us, and then guides us into its practical expression. This wisdom also comes from prayerful asking (James 1:5).

Many years ago in my morning time with the Lord, the Spirit deeply convicted me that I had not loved my wife Gerrie like Christ loves the Church. Oh, I had loved her but not like He wanted me to. He commands husbands to love their wives as Christ loved the Church and gave Himself up for her (Ephesians 5:25). This is an incredible sacrificial love, far beyond human capability. I specifically committed myself to obey Him in this matter knowing full well that He must enable me to do so. How could I love Gerrie this way without Him? It was a deliberate choice on my part to obey as an act of faith. However, I did not know how to love her this way. What would it look like? How would it be different from the love she had known from me for ten or eleven years. I then told the Lord that I did not know how. Would He please show me what to do to express His kind of love to Gerrie? Would He fill me with His love for her? It was sealed in my heart that I wanted her to know Christ's sacrificial love through me as her husband all the days of her life, or as long as I lived. The Spirit had applied scriptural truth to my heart convicting me. I had responded with godly sorrow and deep repentance to my Lord and to Gerrie. Now He must show me how to walk it out. Throughout these last thirty-plus years, He has guided me in specific ways by putting thoughts into my head and heart regarding what I should do to express Christ's love to Gerrie, things I would never have thought of doing or saying on my own. This has brought joyous fulfillment to my heart beyond my highest imagination. The Word obeyed through the strength of the Spirit always does.

The first prompting by the Spirit happened one day when I was in our bedroom packing my suitcase for a speaking trip. Suddenly there came this thought, "Thank Gerrie for having your clothes clean, folded, and ready for packing." I knew this was the Holy Spirit leading me because I would not have normally thought of this. I turned to her and said, "Thank you, Gerrie, for washing my clothes and having them ready." She was quite surprised and remembers to this day where she was standing in our bedroom when I spoke to her. The Holy Spirit also led me into new ways of expressing acceptance and approval for her by words and actions instead of being critical and harsh, and to serve her instead of always expecting her to serve me and take care of me. These were not big things, but rather simple things, like always opening the door for her to get into the car when we were going somewhere. Step by step the Spirit has led the way in *agape* love's practical expression.

Ephesians and Colossians were companion letters written by Paul at the same time but sent to two different places. In many ways the letters are similar even though they were written for different purposes. The section in Ephesians 5:18–20 has a parallel in Colossians 3:16–17. Ephesians 5:18 commands us "to be filled with the Spirit." Colossians 3:16 commands, "Let the word of Christ richly dwell within you." In both places the verbs mean to continue in these commands. Keep on being filled with the Spirit, and keep on letting the Word richly dwell in you. Throughout the Bible, beginning in Genesis 1:2–3, we see that the Word of God and the Spirit of God work together. You cannot neglect the Word and be filled with the Spirit. Fullness by the Spirit and richness in the Word go together. The Bible teaches us how we are to live for God's glory and the Spirit reveals it to our hearts. He then shows us how to apply it very precisely in daily life, and by His fullness empowers us to walk out it out.

Dr. Packer wrote, "And his own (Paul's) triumphant cry from prison as he faces possible execution is: 'I can do all things [meaning, all that God calls me to do] in him who *strengthens* me' (Philippians 4:13). There is no mistaking the thrust of all this. What we are being told is that supernatural living through supernatural empowering is at the very heart of New Testament Christianity, so that those who, while professing faith, do not experience and show forth this empowering are suspect by New Testament standards. And the empowering is always the work of the Holy Spirit, even when Christ only is named as its source, for Christ is the Spirit giver (John 1:33, 20:22, Acts 2:33)."[4]

Doing the Next Thing

When your heart is absolutely surrendered, and you are depending on the Lord to guide you, then you can trust Him to put His thoughts into your thinking and infuse His desires into your desires or change them. Philippians 2:13 promises, "For it is God who is at work in you, both to will and to work for His good pleasure." Another translation says it well, "For God is working in you, giving you the desire to obey him and the power to do what pleases him" (NLT). Believers should not wait passively for the Lord to tell them what they should do. He has given us a mind that He expects us to use. He has promised to direct our steps if we trust Him rather than ourselves, and seek Him in all we do (Proverbs 3:5–6). He declares quite clearly that He ordains our steps (Proverbs 20:24). In Acts 16:6–7 (quoted in the epigraph) Paul had a plan but the Spirit directed his steps a different way than he had planned. In Romans 1:13 Paul said, "Often I have planned to come to you (and have been prevented so far)." As Christians we should plan for what we are responsible to do and faithfully do it with all our heart as to the Lord (Colossians 3:23). Ecclesiastes 9:10 instructs, "Whatever your hand finds to do, do it with all your might." When God wants to redirect your steps in the midst of walking out your plan, He will. When we are wholly His and trust Him, we can rest with assurance that He is guiding us as we fulfill our responsibilities, doing the next thing we know to do.

When our son Jeff was newly married and living in Florida, almost twenty years ago, he worked construction, building houses during the day, and attending college on certain nights to finish his degree in business management. On a rare and unusually cold, dark, rainy night for Florida, he went to the store. He wore a sweatshirt for warmth. As he drove up the highway past a strip mall, he glanced over at the stores and from the parking lot lights saw a young African-American man standing in the doorway of a closed store with no shirt on, his arms folded across his chest, enduring the cold. Jeff said that as he drove past he knew God spoke to him, "Give him your shirt." It was a dual highway, so he drove to the next crossover, turned around and went back to where he had seen the man. The man was still standing there in the cold, damp air with his arms folded across his chest trying to stay warm. My son took off his sweatshirt, rolled the passenger side window down, and handed it to the man without saying a word. The young man took it and said thank you. Jeff said that as he drove off, he looked in his rear view mirror and saw the man putting it on. He said, "I knew the shirt was still warm from my body as he it put on his own body." Jesus said, "[I was] naked and you clothed me . . . Truly I say to you, to the extent that you did it to one of these brothers of Mine, even the least of them, you did it to Me" (Matthew 25:36, 40). To stay in step with the Spirit we must obey His Word, do the next thing, and follow those inner promptings that apply what He said. Otherwise we quench the Spirit.

Keeping in step with the Spirit is not just for ministry purposes but also for practical living, like caring for children, serving your wife, honoring your husband, doing your work to please the Lord, cleaning house, maintaining your yard, dressing appropriately, grocery shopping, doing business, paying your bills, driving your car. Simply stated, it is for all of life's ingredients.

What kind of carpenter do you think Jesus was? What kind of son would He have been to His mother? How would He have kept His workshop? What kind of neighbor would His neighbors have thought Him to be? What kind of businessman would He have been? We seldom consider the fact that before His extraordinary three years of public ministry, Jesus spent many years living an ordinary daily existence. Was He filled with the Spirit in those silent years?

Did He glorify His heavenly Father in those quiet ordinary days as much as He did when multitudes came to Him? Of course! He was always filled with the Spirit without measure and all that He did was under the Spirit's control. Every moment He was in step with the Spirit. Jesus was God in a human body living a very human daily life depending on the same Spirit He has given for us to live by. All of His life—His ordinary daily existence for three decades as well as His powerful, brief years of ministry—glorified His Father.

Following Inner Promptings

Normally you should live by, what I call, sanctified common sense. With God's Word richly abiding in you, and having a willing, trusting heart, you should make your plans and decisions with confidence that the Lord is guiding you. There will be occasions, however, when special inner promptings come that are quiet and persistent. These inner urgings will not be loud, boisterous, demanding, or threatening. They will not come shrouded with fear but clothed with loving gentleness. They will always be in line with God's Word, never contrary to it. These inner leadings are never for selfish reasons and desires, nor is the motive ever for pride or praise of self. Their purpose is usually for the purpose of some ministry Jesus wants to accomplish through you. The distinct persistent impression upon your heart will lead you to do something that expresses God's pure and holy love to someone in need. Sometimes you will not even be aware of their need, but as you obey, there will come the glad knowledge that indeed the Holy Spirit led you. The effect will be blessing for another and honor for Christ. It will bring praise to God, and at times, even joyous awe. You will be encouraged by God's faithfulness to direct your steps, even beyond your normal reasoning process. Jesus said, "My sheep hear [continuously] my voice, and I know [continuously] them, and they follow [continuously] Me" (John 10:27).

Sometimes people say to me, "I'm afraid I will not hear His voice or understand what He wants me to do." Neglecting regular time alone with your Father, along with distractions by pressing external factors, will dull your sensitivity to His voice and cause you to ignore His impressions upon your heart. God is the original communicator. He knows exactly how to speak clearly to your heart, and, furthermore, He knows what it will take for you to hear and to listen. That is no problem for Him. However, the responsibility rests with you to maintain close communion with your Father and always be ready to do His bidding. If you should miss it sometimes, it is good to remember that we are mere children growing up who must learn how to walk in constant communion with the Spirit. Our failures are a part of our discipleship training, and our loving heavenly Father does not forsake us if we "miss it." He uses our failures to correct us and teach us. If we are humble and teachable, then He is pleased, and we can leave all the consequences in His hands.

An African-American friend, who was a deacon in a nearby Baptist church (and is now with the Lord), took me to meet his pastor. Pastor Miller, who is a little older than I, is a distinguished-looking man with graying hair. Upon meeting and talking with him, I learned that he grew up in Virginia, my home state. He lived in the east side of Virginia in the tidewater region. I grew up in the southwestern part of the state in the mountains. We both ended up in Louisiana. He asked if I would come preach in his church one Sunday. I was delighted. Many in our church wanted to reach out across racial lines to break down walls and build bridges between the races. This was another small step in the right direction. The history of race relations between African-Americans and whites in our deep-south town has not been good in past years, although better in more recent times. Prejudice cannot exist in a heart full of God's love any more than germs can live in a bottle of alcohol. Christians give powerful witness to the gospel of Jesus Christ when they love brothers and sisters regardless of color or nationality or culture. I cannot find any reference to skin color in Scripture. In Bible times people were identified by where they came from.

Some people from my church accompanied me as I went to deliver the sermon in this African-American church. It was an excellent time for getting to know one another and for worshiping together. We were warmly received.

Pastor Miller invited me again to come to his church to speak, and I gladly accepted. While praying and thinking about what I was to speak about this time, I settled on the passage in John 4:1–26. Jesus did not go around Samaria, as many other Jews did because of strong prejudice against the Samaritans, but rather He went through it in order to minister there. As I prepared the message and prayed, I kept having an inner impression. For several days the impression remained with me, "Wash Pastor Miller's feet." We both had grown up in an era when segregation was strong. I remember as a young boy riding the city bus and reading the sign painted at the front above the windshield, "Whites to front. Colored to rear." African-Americans were referred to as "colored people" then. I recall going to the football stadium and seeing restrooms, one for whites and another for "colored." The water fountains were marked the same way. "Colored people" could not go into any restaurant to eat, but only to those willing to serve them. Those kinds of distinctions fed the wicked pride and deceptive feelings of white superiority. There were no blacks in any of the schools I attended until seminary. There were none in any of the churches I attended. I look back with shame at those years and still feel sadness when I think of it. It was terribly wrong, but it was the prevailing attitude in the South at that time. Pastor Miller grew up under those conditions. No doubt prejudice had wounded him and left deep scars. "Wash his feet." I could not get away from the thought. "But how will it be received? Will it embarrass him? Will it be foolish and presumptuous on my part? What will his congregation think?" Yet, I began to believe that indeed the Lord was speaking to me, that this persistent, gentle, inner impression was the Spirit directing me.

I asked some of the men who were going with me to make preparations. We needed a large washbowl filled with water and a towel. I asked one of their deacons to be prepared to bring a chair down in front of the platform after I finished speaking. After the message I took Pastor Miller by the hand and led him down the steps and around to the center in front of the pulpit. As we approached the chair where he would sit, I said to him, "Pastor Miller, I want to wash your feet." He immediately burst into tears and cried. I had him sit down. I took off my coat, laid it across the back of one of the pews, and rolled up my shirtsleeves. The men brought the large bowl filled with water and I got down to wash his feet. I was deeply moved with compassion for him because of all the hurt he had endured through years of prejudice by whites against the race to which He belonged. He continued to weep harder, even out loud, with his head back as if looking up to heaven. The people in the congregation, both black and white, began to cry. Someone began quietly singing the one word chorus, "Alleluia," and others joined in. It was one of those unforgettable moments, a holy moment in the Lord's presence. It was like we all had been washed by heaven. Suppose I had not followed that quiet, persistent, and gentle inward prompting upon my heart? I would have missed the joy of seeing Jesus be who He is. We would have missed seeing His glory.

Keeping in step with the Spirit means to follow His lead wherever to do whatever while leaving the consequences with your Lord. Sometimes it will seem risky, humanly speaking, and it will be. However, you will have the superlative joy of seeing Him work in response to your faith and obedience.

Sometimes the Spirit calls us to do something we would not especially want to do. He puts us in places of dependence on Him, places that generate helpless feelings. He will lead us beyond our normal level of comfort and convenience. He wants us to learn well the central lesson of abandonment with total dependence upon Him. The Spirit leads us in ways that will conform us to Christ. He will stretch us in faith, hope, and love, and that cannot be done without putting us in situations and relationships where we have to exercise those qualities. These three attitudes—faith, hope, and love—governed the life of Jesus, and we must learn to walk as He walked. And, indeed, it is a learning process.

A few years ago a missionary in a Middle Eastern Muslim country asked if there were any men from our church who would volunteer to go with him into an unevangelized and difficult region of that country to search out how best to get the gospel there. Our church had adopted this Muslim country as a missionary target. Five men stepped forward. Each of them had families. They would take vacation days from their jobs, spend thousands of dollars, and go. It would be a fairly dangerous mission. We set up a prayer ministry to surround them for their journey. This was a new place for us in missions as a church and would definitely stretch our faith. The day came for their departure, and we entered those ten days with apprehension, but trusting that they would return safely with their mission accomplished.

They arrived and the missionaries told them the plans had been changed. It was too dangerous for them to go into the northern region as had been planned. They would stay in the south and do other things. Deep disappointment came over the men and they each said with tears, "We have come prepared for any consequences. We must go there." Arrangements were then made to carry out the original planned mission.

The government would not let them go without a military escort, which was a truck with seven Arab warriors, each with an AK-47. A fifty-caliber machine gun was mounted on the back of the truck, and a rocket launcher was in the floorboard. Our son Jeff was one of the men who went, and he said that these men were the hardest men he had ever seen. Yet, the Spirit impressed him to ask if he could get in the truck and ride with them. The officer in charge put him up front in the middle. Then later some of the other men got in the back of the truck with the other soldiers. By this simple gesture of friendship, doors were opened for a witness about Jesus.

Before the mission trip Jeff kept thinking, "You will meet a powerful Arab sheikh. Buy an expensive knife to give him as a gift." The thought persisted, so he went and bought an expensive knife to take with him. He deeply believed the Lord had impressed this on his heart, and he left on the trip convinced that he would indeed meet a powerful Arab sheikh.

On their journey through the northern region, they came to a village where they saw some young Arab men playing volleyball. One of our men said, "Let's stop and play volleyball with them." And they did. Neither group could speak the other's language, except for the missionary leading the team, but they played ball together. During their game a car drove up with an older man seated in the passenger side. The driver got out, came to the passenger's door, and stood there. Jeff thought he should go over and speak to the older man seated in the car, even though he could not speak Arabic. He approached the car, not knowing how the man by the door would respond, and greeted the man seated in the car. The older man returned the greeting. He then got out of the car and spoke with the team leader. From their conversation they learned that this was the Arab sheikh Jeff had expected he would meet. The sheikh invited these Americans to dinner. At the appointed time they arrived and were warmly received. They had a lovely dinner in the home of this powerful leader and ruler. After dinner Jeff got up, went over to the sheikh, and said through the interpreter, "I thought when I came to visit your country, I was going to meet a very important man. I brought you this gift," and handed him the knife. The sheikh was very surprised, and then reciprocating, gave Jeff a knife in a silver sheath. It was the style of knife like each man in that country wears. What Jeff did not realize, as he followed this inner prompting to buy the knife for a sheikh, was that in this country they value American knives greatly, and this was the perfect gift. To tell the whole story would be a book in itself.

After Jeff returned from the first trip, he came to me one Sunday night after church and said, "I've got to go back." As his father I did not want to see him go back into this dangerous zone again. I asked why. He said with tears in his eyes, "Somebody has to tell the sheikh about Jesus. I must go even if I must go alone." You cannot teach your children to walk with God and to do His will—no matter the cost—and then resist when their obedience to what they believe is the will of God makes *you* uncomfortable. My task was to encourage, support, and pray. Jeff planned his next trip and went again with some other men who decided to go with him. Since then several follow-up trips have been made to this region. The men always go into this area with armed protection from the sheikh's men, and most recently by the government's soldiers, because of the danger within the region. They were there on September 11, 2001, during the terrorist attacks and were carefully protected by the sheikh's armed men until they could get out of the country.

In subsequent trips Jeff, and the men with him, have shared the gospel with the sheikh and some of his family. They have given him an Arabic-English Bible. They have also had question-and-answer sessions with him about the gospel and about what he had read in his Bible. One time they had a very honest discussion in front of several Muslim men. Jeff has even taken his wife and fifteen-year-old son Jeffrey with him to visit this grandfather figure who has since become a dear friend. They were treated with utmost kindness and respect by everyone.

On Jeff's most recent trip, one of the sheikh's adult sons had been having severe long-term headaches that no medication would affect. Jeff sensed an inner desire and urging to ask if he could pray for this Muslim friend. Immediately there was a tension that could be felt from the several men in the room. This was an American Christian, whom Muslims consider to be infidels, asking if he could pray for the sheikh's son. The sheikh's son thought for a moment, and then said, "Yes." So Jeff stepped forward, placed his hands on the man's head, and prayed in Jesus' Name for him to be healed. Their Muslim interpreter translated. This was not a usual practice for Jeff. When the prayer was finished, the Muslim interpreter said in English to a missionary standing nearby, "What was that? Did you feel that? There was something above us while he prayed." Jeff had also felt the presence above them and almost stopped to look up to see what it was. The headache left. When the team left the country, there had been no more headaches. The man said, "My headaches left when you prayed for me." Those Muslim men will have to reckon with the power of Jesus' Name, power that Allah does not have. How important it is to follow those inner promptings by the Spirit. It opens the door for Him to work for Christ's glory.

Each mission trip is an awe-inspiring experience as these businessmen witness what God is accomplishing for His kingdom when they obey the Spirit's promptings. As I write this they are preparing to go again this month.

Keeping in step with the Spirit leads to places of ministry your flesh would not naturally want to go. It may not be to some foreign land. It may be in your neighborhood, or your church, or a hospital, or an inner-city ministry, or any one of countless possibilities. As you follow Him in obedience and see God do His unexplainable and unexpected work, you catch glimpses of His glory. Your love for Him increases. Your reward is a deep fulfillment that comes from being in your Father's will and seeing Him do what only He can do. Deep overflowing joy comes from being an expression of heaven's love for the sake of advancing God's kingdom in this world. Becoming

Christ-like in your character and expressing His love and compassion to those in need is the purpose of the Spirit's fullness. Only this quality of life is unexplainable because it is God Himself filling and doing His extraordinary work through ordinary human beings. God is going to accomplish His work for His kingdom. It is up to you—and me—to decide if we want to be an instrument He can use. Only the Spirit's fullness and anointing qualifies us to be an effective instrument in His hand. Walking in line with Him is the way.

John 5:19 records Jesus' words, "Truly, truly, I say to you, the Son can do nothing of Himself, unless it is something He sees the Father doing; for whatever the Father does, these things the Son also does in like manner." This is how Jesus kept in step with the Spirit. He spent adequate time alone with His Father in order to hear His will and do it. As He walked through His days, His heart's inner eye was always looking to the Father in faith. By His earthly life He showed us the way to live and is our example to follow.

This is not difficult to do, but it does require making the choice to do it. Tozer wrote, "Now, if faith is the gaze of the heart at God, and if this gaze is but the raising of the inward eyes to meet the all-seeing eyes of God, then it follows that it is one of the easiest things possible to do. It would be like God to make the most vital thing easy and place it within the range of possibility for the weakest and poorest of us."[5]

Often Christians are so occupied with outward practical matters such as daily responsibilities, schedules, and needs—what Jesus calls "the worry of the world" (Matthew 13:22)—that the clamor of external concerns drowns out the quiet inner voice of the Spirit. Ordering your priorities by deliberate and sometimes hard choices is absolutely essential if you want to stay in step with the His Spirit. You will need regular and unhurried time alone with the Lord for worship, meditation in God's Word, and prayer. Neglecting intimate communion with your Lord guarantees spiritual failure in your walk. That is why the enemy, who walks about seeking whom he may devour (1 Peter 5:8), relentlessly pursues you in order to distract you by worldly occupations. Jealously guard your time alone with your heavenly Father like Jesus did.

Archbishop Leighton (1611–1684), Archbishop of Glasgow, Scotland, said, "The sum is: Remember always the presence of

God; rejoice always in the will of God; and direct all to the glory of God."[6] Theodore Monod, a French Christian author, said, "All is in Christ, by the Holy Spirit, for the glory of God. All else is nothing."[7] This is why we must keep in step with the Spirit.

All-glorious and loving heavenly Father,

You are worthy of no other gift than my complete abandonment to You every day. I cannot live worthy of Your Name except as I experience Your Spirit's fullness and follow His leading. When You gave me new life, You planted in me the desire to become like Jesus, and I cannot be satisfied except as I know that I am growing in His likeness. I long to be like You, not only in character, but also by being an expression of Your compassionate love to those You give to me. I need Your fullness. Oh, how I need Your fullness in order to accurately represent Jesus by ministering His life. Please use me as Your instrument to increase Your kingdom in this world. Teach me Your ways, my Lord, and lead me in all the paths You have for me. I want, as strongly as I know how, for all of my life to bring glory and honor to You forever and ever. Amen!

Notes

[1] W. E. Vine, *The Expanded Vine's Expository Dictionary of New Testament Words*, (Minneapolis, Minnesota: Bethany House Publishers, 1984), 1207.

[2] Packer, *Knowing God*, 11.

[3] Sanders, *Enjoying Intimacy with God*, 83–84.

[4] Packer, *Keep in Step with the Spirit*, 23.

[5] A. W. Tozer, *The Pursuit of God*, (Harrisburg, Pennsylvania: Christian Publications, Inc.), 94.

[6] Source unknown.

[7] Source unknown.

CHAPTER SEVEN

Exceptional Fillings by the Spirit

*And when they had prayed, the place where they
had gathered together was shaken, and they were
all filled with the Holy Spirit and began to speak the
Word of God with boldness.*
—Acts 4:31

In my late twenties I traveled with some other men by car from our
home in Virginia to North Carolina to attend a conference where
some well-known preachers were speaking. Dr. Stephen Olford,
who was Senior Pastor of Calvary Baptist Church in New York City,
spoke in the morning session. I had heard him speak once previously at another conference. This time, however, there was power
in his preaching like I had never witnessed before. Men, probably
two thousand of them, were deeply moved and many wept because
the Holy Spirit was so powerfully present. I later learned that there
had been much prayer for the conference. That night Dr. Olford
preached again, and this time the anointing that had been upon his
preaching in the late morning session was like a double portion for

the night session. The power upon his preaching put me, and others, into another realm, and I was in a spiritual place I had never experienced before. Time was suspended in the presence of God, and our hearts were deeply stirred as truth powerfully confronted us. He spoke in the evening session about the necessity of the fullness of the Holy Spirit for life and ministry and illustrated it from his own testimony and that of Billy Graham. I was witnessing a demonstration of the very thing he was preaching. As a young pastor that formative experience was used to encourage me further about this vital truth regarding my absolute need for the power of the Holy Spirit for my life and ministry.

Dr. Olford was a very energetic, winsome, and dynamic preacher with biblically powerful sermons, but this was beyond the usual. No doubt, this was an exceptional anointing (fullness) by the Holy Spirit.

I returned home and tried to describe to my wife what I had witnessed. Of course, how could she understand what I tried to describe? Neither of us had ever experienced anything like it before. It was one of those times when you just had to be there. The next summer I took my wife and our two small children to a summer conference where Dr. Olford regularly spoke each summer. Thursday night of the weeklong conference, Dr. Olford brought a message on the filling of the Holy Spirit. Once again, the Holy Spirit gave witness to the truth with extraordinary power. I glanced at my wife during the message and saw that she was being affected as I had been in the previous conference. After the meeting I said to her outside, "That is what I was telling you about." She replied, "I could not understand. It is indescribable." Indeed it was. It was none other than the presence of Jesus revealed in power by an exceptional filling of the Spirit.

I was eager to learn all I could about the powerful work of the Holy Spirit in ministry. I knew so little, and did not know how to distinguish between the different aspects of the Holy Spirit's ministry. I continued searching for answers regarding this mysterious work of the Spirit.

Special Fillings

Continuing my search, I finally came to understand that there is a difference between fullness for daily life and exceptional filling for special ministry.

Jesus' disciple, Simon Peter, was filled with the Spirit on the day of Pentecost, just as Jesus had promised all His disciples (Acts 1:8). With that fullness came the power necessary to proclaim the good news, and Peter gave a powerful witness of Jesus Christ to the Jews present, as did the others (Acts 2:5–36). Later Peter and John were the instruments God used to heal miraculously a lame man at the gate called Beautiful. That opened a wonderful opportunity to proclaim Jesus Christ to the crowd that gathered. This stirred up the Jewish leaders who were against Jesus and His followers, and Peter and John were put on trial before the hostile Jewish Council for proclaiming Jesus. Peter was already filled by the Spirit poured out on the day of Pentecost (Acts 2), but Dr. Luke records in Acts 4:8, "Then Peter, filled with the Holy Spirit, said to them . . ." The verb *filled* in the original language can be translated, "Peter *having just been filled* with the Holy Spirit." If he was already filled, then why was he filled again at this moment? He was exceptionally filled with the Spirit for this time of special need (Luke 21:14–15). The Jewish Council commanded Peter and John not to speak or teach at all in the name of Jesus. Peter and John answered them and said, "Whether it is right in the sight of God to give heed to you rather than to God, you be the judge" (Acts 4:19). The Council threatened them and then released them "finding no basis on which to punish them" (Acts 4:21). They returned to their fellow believers and reported what had been said to them. Upon hearing this, the church lifted up their voices with one accord and prayed (Acts 4:24–31). In their prayer they worshiped God, acknowledged the opposition against them because of Jesus, affirmed God's sovereignty, asked for boldness to keep on speaking God's Word, and asked God to confirm it with miracles. At the end of their prayer, "the place where they had gathered together was shaken and they were all filled with the Holy Spirit and began to speak the word of God with boldness" (Acts 4:31). Again, Peter was present for this *special filling by the Holy*

Spirit, which equipped the disciples to proclaim the gospel boldly in the face of the religious leaders' threats.

The Bible reports another time of an exceptional filling by the Holy Spirit. The Holy Spirit told the leaders in the church at Antioch during a time of worshiping and fasting to set apart Barnabas and Saul (Paul) for the work to which He had called them (Acts 13:1–3). They were set apart with prayer, fasting, and laying-on of hands. These two plus John Mark set out on their first missionary journey. They came to the island of Paphos. Sergius Paulus, the governor, wanted to hear the word of God from Saul and Barnabas and sent for them to come before him. A Jewish magician named Bar-Jesus, also known as Elymas, was with the governor. Elymas opposed these missionaries and tried to turn the governor away from the truth they were preaching. The account reads, "But Saul, who was also known as Paul, *filled with the Holy Spirit*, fixed his gaze on him" (italics added), and told him that the Lord would temporarily blind him (Acts 13:9–11). Just like it was with Peter in Acts 4:8, the verb translation is more accurate when we read it, *"having just been filled with the Holy Spirit."* A. T. Robertson, an outstanding Greek scholar of the last century, calls this type of filling "a special influx of power to meet this emergency."[1] This was an exceptional filling beyond the usual fullness for everyday life.

There are other places in the book of Acts where an exceptional fullness of the Spirit for ministry is evident. For example, people brought the sick and afflicted and laid them on cots and pallets in the street "so that at least Peter's shadow might fall on any one of them" (Acts 5:15). Philip, the deacon, preached in Samaria and miraculous signs accompanied him (Acts 8:5–6), indicating an unusual anointing. Acts contains other places where exceptional manifestations of the Spirit's presence and power occur. Pentecost was probably an exceptional filling of the Spirit in addition to His normal indwelling and fullness.

In several places the Bible speaks of the Holy Spirit coming *upon* an individual or a group. The Greek preposition *upon* is used in Luke 24:49; Acts 1:8; 2:3, 17; 4:33; 8:16; 10:44; 11:15; and 19:6. Jesus used three prepositions—*in, with,* and *upon*—to teach about the Holy Spirit's relationship with His followers. I don't think the prepositions can be used to make clear-cut doctrinal distinctions between various experiences with the Holy Spirit. These prepositions seem to be descriptive terminology rather than doctrinal or theological terms. Therefore, different orthodox evangelicals call the exceptional filling of the Spirit by different terms. Men like Dr. Martyn Lloyd-Jones, R. A. Torrey, Charles G. Finney, Oswald Chambers, and others have used the term *baptism of the Spirit*. Others may use the term *anointing* or *filling* by the Spirit. I prefer to use the term *filling* for the fullness of the Holy Spirit for daily life, and the term *anointing* for the fullness of the Spirit *upon* someone for ministry. Jesus called this anointing being "clothed with power from on high" (Luke 24:49). The anointing can occur in varying degrees according to God's sovereign choice. However, should we quibble over terms when what we so desperately need is the Holy Spirit of God filling us and being poured out upon us to clothe us with power from on high? We should be as doctrinally accurate as possible with the use of Bible terms, but we can be theologically correct and yet lack the reality of the Spirit's fullness and anointing in our lives. Only as we have the reality of these gifts will we see the amazing ministry of the Holy Spirit doing the unexplainable and unexpected works of God in our midst.

Jesus always possessed the Spirit in fullness for His ordinary life until He was thirty, but now at His baptism the Spirit came *upon* Him to anoint Him for the beginning of His public ministry (Luke 3:22). At the end of His three-year public ministry as He was about to go back to His Father, He told the disciples that the same Spirit would come *upon* them and they were to wait to begin their ministry of world evangelization until this occurred (Luke 24:49, Acts 1:8). The Spirit poured out on them at Pentecost gave them the anointing of the Spirit upon them, the indwelling of the Spirit within them, and the empowering by the Spirit filling them. All three occurred at once. That doesn't usually happen with us.

Dr. Martyn Lloyd-Jones in his book, *Joy Unspeakable,* is very helpful when he writes:

> The baptism with the Spirit belongs to the category
> of the exceptional and direct. This brings us to the

characteristics of the baptism with the Spirit . . . The great term is 'poured out.' This, of course, suggests at once a great profusion—and this is what we must emphasize. The Spirit came upon them as he came upon our Lord. He came upon those people who were assembled together in the upper room. If you like, you can describe it almost as a kind of 'drenching with the Spirit' . . .

People seem to think that this is some strange new doctrine. It is very old indeed, as old as the New Testament, and it has received prominence in the church throughout the centuries. There is an illustration which may help to bring out this point. You may be walking along a country road and there may be a slight drizzle, but because you haven't got an overcoat you go on walking through this drizzle and eventually you get thoroughly wet, but it has taken some time because it was only a slight drizzle. But then you may be walking along the same road at another time and suddenly there is a cloudburst and you are soaking wet in a matter of seconds. It is raining in both cases, but there is a great difference between a gentle drizzle, which you scarcely observe, and a sudden cloudburst which comes down upon you.[2]

God commands us to be filled with the Spirit (Ephesians 5:18), and that means I have some control over that. I can obey God's command by cooperating with Him according to the means outlined from His Word (as I mentioned in Chapter 4), but the exceptional filling (anointing) by the Spirit is totally under God's sovereign control. Not only does He choose when and to what degree the Spirit should be upon His servant, but He chooses which servant He will use for His purpose. For example, why was it Paul rather than Barnabas that received a special influx of power to confront Elymas the magician who opposed them (Acts 13:9–11)? It was God's sovereign choice. You can drink of His fullness like drinking water, but you cannot grasp the anointing just as you cannot grasp oil. (Oil is often used in the Bible as a symbol for anointing.) We cooperate for the Spirit's fullness through faith and obedience, but for anointing (exceptional fullness) all we can do is to remain available for the moment when God chooses to impart it. We are available when we live continually full of the Spirit, listen so we can hear the Spirit's guidance, and cooperate with Him by simple obedience.

Tony Sargent in his book, *The Sacred Anointing*, writes, "In other words, this effusion hinges entirely upon the sovereign will of the Holy Spirit. He may grant it, he may not. It is utterly at his discretion. Receiving it once does not mean you can bank on it the next time."[3] This keeps us in the place of humility and dependence. Furthermore, this keeps us asking, seeking, and knocking because God alone can give the anointing we so desperately need for ministering the life of Jesus to others regardless of what our ministry might be.

A few years ago I was having lunch with a dear older, respected brother who had served as a missionary in Japan for many years. We were guest speakers for a summer conference that would begin that evening. He looked across the table and asked me, "Do you get nervous before you speak?" I replied quite honestly, "Helpless!" He chuckled, but I was very serious. Without God's anointing it is just words. It may be truth, but truth can be lifeless. Jesus said, "It is the Spirit who gives life; the flesh profits nothing; the words that I have spoken to you are spirit and are life" (John 6:63). Only the Spirit can make our preaching, singing, praying, witnessing, testifying, or whatever breathe with the actual life of Jesus. Without that sense of urgency in our souls, we will pray our usual prayers for God's blessing and do what we always do, but miss having those times of His revealed presence and active power. I believe the ministry of Jesus' Word should not only be the exposition of His truth but the ministry of His Life. That only happens when the spokesman is filled and anointed by the Holy Spirit.

I have a dear friend I mentored who is like a son in ministry and holds a position of professor of New Testament Interpretation at Southern Baptist Theological Seminary in Louisville, Kentucky. In a phone conversation one day Dr. Bill Cook said, "Jerry, there is much expositional preaching today but little with anointing." This is a sad state for the Church. When "king self" rules with its pride, the Spirit of Christ is hindered. We must be at the place of humility and whole-hearted dependence if we will be useful for God to anoint. Those who hear the truth proclaimed, both believers and non-believers, need to encounter the living Christ, and only the Spirit's fullness and anointing can cause this to happen.

Leigh Powell in the book, *Chosen by God*, said about Dr. Martyn Lloyd-Jones' ministry: "At times, often toward the end of the sermon, he seemed to be hovering, waiting for something . . . sometimes the wind of the Spirit would come and sweep us and him aloft and we would mount with wings like eagles into the awesome and felt presence of God."[4] Note the word "sometimes." It does not occur every time, but it does occur sometimes, and should happen more often than it does in many church services.

In 1972 I was invited to Greenville, South Carolina to speak in a series of meetings. I was young and inexperienced and felt extremely unqualified for such an assignment. The church was well taught, mature, and among the members was a well-known Bible teacher. I approached this assignment feeling intimidated. I decided to go to a mountain cabin to pray and seek the Lord regarding the upcoming meetings. As I began my trip, I was praying while I drove. Suddenly the presence of the Lord came upon me. I drove and wept and prayed. This lasted for a long while, and I was hardly conscious of anything else except the Lord and His presence. I did not understand at the time what was happening to me, but I look back now with better understanding and realize that this was the Spirit coming upon me for preaching in those meetings. It was the first time I consciously experienced the Holy Spirit coming upon me, even though I did not understand its significance at the time. This kind of Spirit preparation is not always a conscious experience. I later learned that there were godly people in the church that had fasted and prayed for three days for the meeting, and no doubt, their fasting and prayers helped prepare me three hundred miles away before I made my journey.

Dan Johnson was a college student then and is now a Bible teacher in The Evangelical Institute of Greenville, South Carolina. He was present in those meetings and gives his testimony about what he saw and experienced:

I remember meetings that never stopped at less than two hours. I remember a sense of the Lord's presence that seemed to hover over every meeting even before the services began. I remember ones near the end of the week that came out of curiosity and criticism (they told me that is why they had come), but their presence did not seem to lessen the impact of the meeting on those who were seeking the Lord. The effects after each message—people streaming to the front weeping, confessing their sins, asking deliverance from various areas of bondage, surrendering to the Lord—did not seem to fit the actual words of the messages. It seemed clear to me at the time that it was not so much the preaching as it was His presence that made the difference.

There was one message, though, that I have never forgotten. I came to the meeting that night very soul weary and spiritually battered having tried to meet the right standards and feeling as though I had fallen so short. The message that night was on the prodigal son and it centered on the love of the Father for the son. The text was simply expounded. The father ran. He fell on his son's neck and kissed him even though he was such an unworthy son. I suddenly felt my heavenly Father greeting me like that. It was hard to accept but inescapable. I began to weep and as I felt His love engulf me, I felt the strain and striving just lift off my shoulders. It was blessed and I have never forgotten it to this day.

There were of course the many who cried out at the front as they were dealt with for demonic problems. Those of us in the pews simply prayed and sang praises to the Lord. I was impressed with people's desperation. They didn't seem to be afraid of being embarrassed or of becoming some sort of spectacle. They simply knew they had a need and wanted it met. Their openness and hunger to be right with God left a strong impression on me that God was at work and that it was time for all of us to mean business with the Lord.

Lest we think that this exceptional filling (or anointing) is only for those in full-time Christian ministry I share a testimony from Dr. Martyn Lloyd-Jones:

> I was in a prayer-meeting once which those of us who were in it will never forget. I remember very well that it was in the month of June. It was a Monday evening prayer-meeting which we had regularly in that church where I was then minister. We had had a remarkable Sunday in many ways, but we came to the meeting as usual and I had called upon somebody to open by reading Scripture and prayer: the meeting started at seven-fifteen. And this man had read the Scripture and had prayed, and another man had got up and prayed in the same way.
>
> Then a third man got up to pray, a man we all knew very well, a simple man, a very ordinary man from the intellectual standpoint. Indeed I must say this, and he would not have resented it; he is no longer alive and his family would not mind. He was a man who had certain defects—as we all do—certain striking defects; a self-important little man, and a man whom we did not in any sense regard as either unusually spiritual or in any other way unusual, and I had heard this man pray many times.
>
> However on this particular evening this man had not uttered more than two or three sentences before I was aware, and everybody else became aware, of something most extraordinary. He was normally halting, humble, pedestrian, ordinary; let me even use the word boring. But suddenly this man was entirely transformed; his voice deepened, a power came into it, even in his speech, and he prayed in

the freest most powerful manner I think I have ever heard in my life.

And you can imagine what happened. The prayer-meeting continued without any intermission, and the freedom that had accompanied this man's prayer was given to all the others. And that went on until nine-fifty. I had not said a word, there was no hymn-singing, there was nothing. It was just this tremendous free power in prayer. One felt that one was outside of time, that one was in heaven; one was really lifted up to the spiritual realm. And here I was listening to people whom I knew so well, praying with freedom and power and assurance; people who had never prayed in public in their lives before, and who had been terrified at the very thought of it, found themselves praying.[5]

Humble, Unworthy Servants

When the seventy disciples of Jesus returned with joy from their mission trips to various villages, they said, "Lord, even the demons are subject to us in Your name (Luke 10:17). Jesus replied, "I was watching Satan fall from heaven like lightning. Behold, I have given you authority to tread on serpents and scorpions, and over all the power of the enemy, and nothing will injure you. Nevertheless do not rejoice in this, that the spirits are subject to you, but rejoice that your names are recorded in heaven" (Luke 10:18–20). He then proceeded to speak about the Father who withholds truth from the proud but reveals it to the humble. The disciples' authority over demons was a gift from the Lord Jesus, and therefore it was not their victory, but His. With just a few words, Jesus put things in true perspective. Their focus must not be on what God does through them, but rather on what God in grace has done for them by saving them.

Jesus said He observed Satan fall from heaven like lightning. In the distant past Satan fell from his high position in heaven in a split second because of pride (Isaiah 14:12–17). In the future, by the authority of Christ, Satan will again fall in a split second from his proud reign as prince of this world into the bottomless pit reserved for him and his demons (Revelation 20:10). God instantly condemned Satan's pride with eternal torment. Because Satan led Adam into sin by temptation to pride, pride is now inherent in our sinful flesh, woven into the very fabric of our beings. One expression of it is craving for credit, recognition, and praise. Our flesh wants to be somebody, whereas Jesus made Himself nothing (Philippians 2:5–8). Mark reports candidly about the disciples, "On the way they had discussed with one another which of them was the greatest." Someone has poignantly observed, "Men always aspire, but God condescends." God's servant can fall as quickly as a lightning strike from the lovely garden of humility into the devil's cesspool of pride. This is why we must walk in cautious, reverent fear.

Paul wrote, "But he who boasts is to boast in the Lord. For it is not he who commends himself that is approved, but he whom the Lord commends" (2 Corinthians 10:17–18). Earlier he wrote, "Neither the one who plants nor the one who waters is anything, but God who causes the growth" (1 Corinthians 3:7). We are God's fellow-workers, but it is God to whom all praise and glory is due. Augustine (AD 354–430) had it right when he wrote, "I was nothing. You had no need of me. Even now my service has not even the value of a laborer tilling his master's land, because even if I did not work, You would bring forth the same harvest. I can only serve You and worship You with the good that comes from You. It is from You alone that I receive strength, and without You I am nothing."[6] By God's grace alone are we His children and only by that same grace is He ever pleased to use us. Therefore all glory, honor, and praise belong to Him. Would we be so foolish as to try to keep any of His glory for ourselves? Any usefulness of any of the Lord's servants is by Him, for Him, and to Him.

As a young pastor, I once commented to a retired missionary about a godly man I had read about who was greatly used by the Lord and said, "What a man!" She quickly replied in her quiet way, "What a Savior!" I understood and was gently corrected. Another wise retired missionary who had been through the Shantung revival in China said, "God will not share His glory with any man." She was right. All God does, whether it be His regular work or His exceptional work, is only for His glory and praise, and no one else's. Who ever honors the surgeon's knife after a successful, delicate surgery? Does the tool ever share the honor of the master craftsman? Is the instrument applauded or the musician at a moving concert? All honor, glory, and praise belong to the one who accomplishes the work. Humility is the first mark of Christ-likeness.

Jesus said, "He [the master] does not thank the slave because he did the things which were commanded, does he? So you too, when you do all the things which are commanded you, say, 'We are unworthy slaves; we have done only that which we ought to have done'" (Luke 17:9–10). Whenever there is an extraordinary work by God's Spirit, the human instruments He uses are no more than unworthy servants because without Him nothing can be done (John 15:5). In moments of exceptional anointing, one easily understands that it is all of Him.

I heard the late Leonard Ravenhill, the British itinerant preacher/ prophet and author who spoke and wrote with powerful effect, tell of a time he was preaching in A. W. Tozer's church in Chicago. He preached for two weeks under an unusual anointing of God's Spirit, an exceptional filling. The last night of the meetings he got up to speak and nothing came out correctly. He stumbled around in his message, got his words mixed up and felt he preached very poorly. The service concluded, and as he and Dr. Tozer were going out the aisle of the church to the entrance to greet the people as they left, Dr. Tozer said to Mr. Ravenhill, "Len, isn't God good?" In relating the story Mr. Ravenhill commented to us, "At that moment I didn't particularly think so." Dr. Tozer continued, "Sometimes God pulls the rug out from under us just to remind us that it is not us, but Him."

As mentioned in the preface, after the healing miracle of the lame man at the gate called Beautiful through Peter and John's ministry, Peter responded to the people's amazement by saying, "Men of Israel, why are you amazed at this, or why do you gaze at us, as if by our own power or piety we had made him walk?" He then plainly told them that this was a work of God in order to glorify Jesus (Acts 3:1–13).

Andrew Murray wrote in his wonderful and convicting book on humility, "When I look back upon my own Christian experience, or at the church of Christ as a whole, I am amazed at how little humility is seen as the distinguishing feature of discipleship. In our preaching and in our living, in our daily interaction in our families and in our social life, as well as fellowship with other Christians, how easy it is to see that humility is not esteemed the cardinal virtue, the root from which grace can grow and the one indispensable condition of true fellowship with Jesus."[7] Dr. Murray further wrote, "There may be enthusiastic and active practice of Christianity while humility is still sadly lacking . . . We find professors and ministers, evangelists and Christian workers, missionaries and teachers, in whom the gifts of the Spirit are many and manifest, and who are the channels of blessing to multitudes, but of whom, when tested, or close interpersonal relationships reveal their true characters, it is only too evident that the grace of humility, as an abiding characteristic, is rarely to be seen."[8]

Octavius Winslow (1808–1878) wrote, "There are three steps in the Christian's life. The first is humility; the second is humility; the third is humility."[9]

Jesus looks for humble vessels He can use to display His glory, and we are commanded to humble ourselves, clothe ourselves with humility, and walk in humility (1 Peter 5:6; Colossians 3:12; Ephesians 4:1–2). Only as you have a clear view of Christ in His perfect beauty, do you gain true knowledge of yourself. True heart-knowledge of the Lord and of yourself leads to humility.

Could pride be preventing us from seeing more of His glory than we do? Pastor Murray points out, "Let us consider how far the disciples were advanced while this grace (humility) was still lacking, and let us pray that other gifts may not so satisfy us that we never grasp the fact that the absence of humility is no doubt the reason why the power of God cannot do its mighty work."[10] We must come to the place where we despise the pride of our own flesh and are repulsed by it. Then holy desperation will propel us to bow humbly before the Lord in our dire neediness. Does any spiritual blessing ever come to us that we do not receive as a gift from our heavenly Father? The Father gives His wondrous gifts to humble ones for His own pleasure and praise.

Whenever the Lord is pleased to use you, and people come to you with various encouragements and compliments, accept their kind words graciously and gratefully as if they had given you flowers.

Then take all of the flowers together as a bouquet and lay them at the feet of Jesus for His pleasure and honor. After all, it is for Him.

Longing for the Spirit

The exceptional filling, or anointing, or pouring out of the Holy Spirit usually occurs where there is deep, sincere longing by humble Christians. God pours out living water where there is thirst like dry land. In China before the Shantung revival the missionaries had noon prayer meetings crying out to God for a moving of His Spirit. Evan Roberts (1878–1951) in Wales, longing for God's Spirit to be poured out, prayed fervently for eleven years until the Spirit fell (1904). In the Hebrides (islands northwest of Scotland) men with great concern for the spiritual condition of the church and their youth met night after night until very late to pray for the Spirit to be poured out. And He came (1949). Dwight L. Moody (1837–1899) became aware of his need for the Holy Spirit's fullness by two ladies in his church who were praying for him. This stirred him to seek for the filling of the Spirit with desperate, persistent prayer until one day in New York City the Spirit powerfully fell upon him. He testified, "I can only say that God revealed Himself to me, and I had such an experience of His love that I had to ask Him to stay His hand." Whenever Charles G. Finney (1792–1875) sensed a lack in his ministry he would go aside and pray for a fresh "baptism of the Spirit," as he would call it. Illustrations abound through Christian history of individuals and groups of people longing for heaven to breathe upon them, and praying until the Father answered and the Wind of heaven blew.

Jesus encourages us about this in Luke 11:1–13. He was teaching the disciples about prayer in response to their request, "Lord, teach us to pray." After teaching them the basics of prayer by what we know as "The Lord's Prayer," He proceeds to teach them another aspect and vital part of prayer by using a parable. A midnight visitor stopped by a certain home for a night's lodging, which was customary in that Middle Eastern culture where there were few lodging places for travelers. It was also a custom of hospitality never to put your traveling guest to bed hungry. This host, however, lacked the necessary bread to feed his guest. It was a moment of desperation. He must not be rude. It would be unthinkable to let his guest go to bed hungry. What must he do? He went to his neighbor, even though the hour was very late. Better to awaken his neighbor at midnight, and perhaps his whole family, than to be embarrassed by poor hospitality. He knocked and knocked until the sleeping neighbor answered from inside. The neighbor thought it too inconvenient to get up and give him what he needed. It must wait until tomorrow. His family asleep in one room, and the door locked with a complicated lock, gave him good reasons to refuse. The host would not receive no for an answer and continued knocking until the neighbor finally got up and granted his request by giving him as much as he needed. The point made in the parable is that humble persistence out of desperate need to an unwilling neighbor finally brought a correct response. Of course, this is a parable of contrast. It is never inconvenient for your heavenly Father to answer, and He most gladly gives what is needed to His humble and urgently seeking ones who continue asking.

Jesus then makes application with strong and repeated assurance. He promises that the Father will answer everyone who keeps on asking, seeking, and knocking (the accurate meaning of the Greek verbs). He then adds an illustration about a father and his son. If his son asks for food, even though the father is a sinful human being, out of fatherly love he will give his son exactly what he needs. How much more will the heavenly Father give what His child asks for?

Then Jesus' application takes a surprising turn. He asks, "How much more will your heavenly Father give the Holy Spirit to those who ask Him?" The Greek verb for "ask," like the asking, seeking, and knocking above, means "keep on asking." The point is quite clear. Like the host, we have absolutely nothing to give from our soul's empty pantry to those who come our way, and therefore we urgently need our Father to supply living bread through the presence, fullness, and power of the Holy Spirit. That is why we must keep on asking for the Holy Spirit from our Father who is so ready and so willing to give.

Leaving Room for the Spirit

If we ask for the Holy Spirit, then we must allow Him to work as He chooses. This threatens some, perhaps even many, because of perceived excesses by others. The watchwords in the Welch revival led by Evan Roberts were "obey the Spirit." An article on the revival says, "On successive nights these meetings drew ever larger crowds, and within a matter of weeks the revival had swept across Glamorganshire with tremendous power. The most significant feature of the revival was its concentration on the gift of the Holy Spirit; the meetings, even when Evan Roberts was present, were conducted with complete spontaneity. People were urged to pray, testify, confess, or sing as the Spirit moved them."[11]

Our pride and fear prevent the Spirit from doing His will. Submission, dependence, and obedience mean that we leave room for the Holy Spirit to operate. If we are afraid of losing control and what will happen if we do, and therefore maintain strict control, then the Holy Spirit cannot be in charge (2 Corinthians 3:17). We forfeit His spontaneity to do the unexpected and unexplainable in our midst for Christ's glory and praise.

Oswald Chambers stated it very clearly:

> As workers for God we have to learn to make room for God—to give God "elbow room." We calculate and estimate, and say that this and that will happen, and we forget to make room for God to come in as He chooses. Would we be surprised if God came into our meeting or into our preaching in a way we had never looked for Him to come? Do not look for God to come in any particular way, but look for Him. That is the way to make room for Him. Expect Him to come, but do not expect Him only in a certain way. However much we may know God, the great lesson to learn is that at any minute He may break in. We are apt to overlook this element of surprise, yet God never works in any other way. All of a sudden God meets the life—"When it pleased God . . ."
>
> Keep your life so constant in its contact with God that His surprising power may break out on the right hand and on the left. Always be in a state of

expectancy, and see that you leave room for God to come in as He likes.[12]

In my last pastorate I was preparing for an Easter Sunday morning service. As I prayed and considered the Lord's will, I kept having a persistent inner impression that I was not to preach an Easter message, or any message. Rather, I was to let the people say or do whatever the Spirit led them to do in order to celebrate our Lord's resurrection day. It was an uneasy and risky place for me to be, but the quiet impression remained. I had always preached an Easter message. It is a great opportunity with all the people who visit on Easter that do not usually come at any other time. Before I settled on what I must do, we prepared an order of service and were scheduled to have an excellent female singer to sing three solos. We went through the first part of the service with congregational worship, including two guest solos, but when the place of the sermon came I said something like, "I am not going to bring a message today. Instead I am going over here and sit down. This service is for our resurrected Lord. You are to minister to Him by whatever you want to say in testimony, Scripture, or song. Microphones are placed on each side of the auditorium and here at the front. Please go to one of the microphones." With that, I took my seat on the front row in one of the side sections, and we waited. There was a short period of quietness, and then someone quietly stood up, went to the microphone, and shared a testimony—so fresh and so real. Another followed, and then another, and so on. Some read Scripture, others gave testimony, and someone else would begin a song of praise with the rest joining in. There came into the room a sense of the Lord's presence like Jesus Himself had walked in. Many tears were shed that day. When our guest soloist came to the platform to sing her third and final song at the end of the service, she had been so deeply stirred to tears that she could not even sing and just returned to her seat. With no one conducting the service but the Holy Spirit, it flowed spontaneously the entire time with many tears of humility and worship. Not once was anything out of order. We left that Easter Sunday fully aware that the resurrected Christ, whose victory over death we celebrated, was manifestly present.

If we long for the Spirit to come, then we must give Him "elbow room" to do as He pleases. "Obey the Spirit."

In the next chapter we will look at the wondrous gift of Jesus' presence revealed for the Father's pleasure and praise.

All-powerful Lord,

> *Your mighty works always amaze us. They reveal Your great mercy and grace through unworthy sinners to unworthy sinners. We know so well that it is only because of the worthiness of Jesus given to us that You are pleased to let us be instruments in Your Hand and be used by You for Your glory.*
>
> *Please forgive us for not being more available to You. We are sorry that we have not been more diligent in seeking You for a greater working of Your Spirit in and through our lives. Please give us a holy dissatisfaction until we long deeply and persistently for a stronger working of Your Spirit among us. You have given us very great promises. We want to believe more than we ever have for the fulfillment of Your great Word. Amen!*

Notes

[1] A. T. Robertson, *Word Pictures in the New Testament,* (Nashville, Tennessee: Broadman Press, 1930), Vol. III, 181.

[2] Martyn Lloyd-Jones, *Joy Unspeakable,* (Wheaton, Illinois: Harold Shaw Publishers, 1985), 67–68.

[3] Tony Sargent, *The Sacred Anointing,* (Wheaton, Illinois: Crossway Books, 1994), 59.

[4] Christopher Catherwood, ed., *Chosen by God,* (Highland Books, Crowborough, 1986), 87.

[5] Lloyd-Jones, *Joy Unspeakable,* 130–131.

[6] Words of Augustine quoted by Nick Harrison, *Magnificent Prayer,* (Grand Rapids, Michigan: Zondervan, 2001), 186.

[7] Andrew Murray, *Humility*, (Minneapolis, Minnesota: Bethany House, 2001), 12.

[8] Ibid., 46.

[9] Octavius Winslow, *Morning Thoughts*, (Grand Rapids, Michigan: Reformation Heritage Books, 2003), 381.

[10] Murray, *Humility*, 49.

[11] R. Tudor Jones, *The New International Dictionary of the Christian Church*, J. D. Douglas, General Editor, (Grand Rapids, Michigan: Zondervan Publishing House, 1974, 1978), 851.

[12] Chambers, *My Utmost for His Highest*, January 25.

CHAPTER EIGHT

Jesus' Presence Revealed

*That nearness is what we are to make daily efforts
after, and that nearness is one capable of indefinite
increase. We know not how close to His heart we
can lay our aching heads. We know not how near to
His fullness we can bring our emptiness. We have
never yet reached the point beyond which
no closer union is possible.*
—Alexander MacLaren

As a young pastor in my late twenties, I was eager to learn all I could about God's presence revealed. As I shared in Chapter 1, it was then that I was awakened to the first possibility of the presence of the Holy Spirit's fullness in the life of the individual believer. During this time, I had read about the revival in northern China in the 1930s. This fresh awareness stirred my heart to understand that the Holy Spirit could descend upon a gathering of Christians anywhere, anytime to reveal Jesus' holy presence. However, as I had observed the churches that were familiar to me, I realized they were not experiencing the revelation of the Holy Spirit's presence in their meetings. I wanted to know about the outpouring of the Spirit known in Christian history as *true revival*. Those were times when God's presence was manifested in powerful ways in various countries and villages.

During the time that I was wrestling with these questions and reading about revivals in Christian history, I participated in a missions conference with a group of Baptist churches in my area. Lucy Wright, a retired missionary nurse, had served in north China during the great outpouring of the Holy Spirit now identified as the Shantung Revival and was to share from her missionary experience with us. This was to be my first opportunity to speak with someone who had actually been present during an outpouring of the Holy Spirit. The outpouring of the Holy Spirit happens when the Person of the Holy Spirit manifests Himself upon a person or a gathering of people, both believers and unbelievers. Although prayer is necessary preparation, He initiates His manifold holy presence at His own discretion. The divine visit is not necessarily because of our requests but can occur as the fruition of the prayers of others who have come before us.

With much anticipation I made an appointment to meet with her. We sat on the sofa in the living room of the home where she was staying, and after a few minutes, I asked her the question burning in my soul, "What was it like?" I will never forget her answer. She said, "The presence of Jesus! The presence of Jesus was so real we would forget to eat. I would walk down the path and meet someone who would ask [and here she spoke a few words in Chinese followed by her translation], 'Have you had your rice yet?' And I would answer, [she put her hand up to her mouth as in surprise] 'No! I forgot.'" As we continued talking, Miss Lucy's testimony helped me begin to grasp what my heart longed to know.

The Lord's presence with His people is that which distinguishes God's people from the rest of the world. "And the sheep follow him because they know his voice" (John 10:4). They know Him. They delight in Him. They enjoy Him. They know His presence is with them. And at moments of His choosing, He makes His presence so real they feel as if they might reach out and touch Him. This is His best gift—Himself. This is our supreme blessing—His drawing so near that we can catch glimpses of His glory.

In this chapter, I will emphasize the magnificent truth that the Holy Spirit still communicates the almost tangible presence of Jesus

Christ in holy moments that only He appoints. However, before I elaborate on those moments, I would like to distinguish these special visitations from the general grace of His presence that He affords all of us who trust in Him. Jesus said in Matthew, "I am with you always, even to the end of the age" (Matthew 28:20). A more accurate translation that reflects the emphasis of the Greek would be, "I *Myself* am with you always." In this passage, Jesus emphatically promises His real, living, and dynamic presence will be with His sheep. In His way, Jesus Himself, through the Holy Spirit, is always present and is everywhere with His own. He is omnipresent, omniscient, and omnipotent. However, special moments also occur during which the Holy Spirit manifests the presence of Jesus in dramatic and intimate ways (John 14:21, 16:12–15).

Because we know the supreme and unchanging nature of Jesus' character (Hebrews 13:8), we are comforted by the knowledge that He is always sovereign, always omniscient, always omnipresent and that for the life of the believer all our hours and moments are superintended by Him. Whether in dramatic or quiet ways, whether through life-changing experiences or subtle revelations—He is indeed always present and near. We need to learn here and now about the Savior who so lovingly discloses Himself to us through His Word and the work of His Holy Spirit.

The Means of His Nearness

The only difference between the presence of Jesus with His disciples when He lived bodily on earth and His presence with them after Pentecost was the means by which He made His presence known. With Jesus' bodily presence on earth, they could touch and see and hear God incarnate. After Pentecost, this same Jesus was present with them, not in His body but by His Spirit. The presence of Jesus would be just as real. They would not be able to touch His flesh, but they would sense His spiritual presence. They would not hear His human voice, but they would know His voice in their inner beings. They would not see His human form, but with the eyes of their hearts they would see His glory. By His Spirit, He would be present with them in larger dimension than He was when He walked with them in the flesh.

When the first church met, they fully expected the Spirit of Jesus to be present in their midst. And He was, as the book of Acts reveals. We can and should anticipate this same experience of Jesus' presence in our individual lives and churches today. When we encounter the shining brightness of Jesus through the presence of the Holy Spirit, all earthly things pale.

David Hazard wrote, "Theresa (of Avila, 1515–1582) agonized all her life, and found it impossible with human language to explain the 'appearances' of Jesus. She 'saw' Him with the eyes of her heart. She caught sight of a new type of beauty that came from of old and extended to everlasting—and a holiness that walked among sinful men, lofty in its intense humility."[1]

Because the Spirit is just like Jesus, He can reveal any facet of Christ's character at any time He chooses. He may unveil for a moment the brightness of Christ's holiness. He may softly speak whispers of compassion. He may have the uncontainable river of Jesus' love wash over you, or He may lead you to a secret sanctuary of His peace. He may startle you with a display of His awesome power. These special visitations of Christ through the means of the Holy Spirit will increase and deepen your love for your Savior and will remind you profoundly of His great sacrifice for you. When your relationship with Christ deepens and grows, it is because He has drawn near and touched your soul. John Piper said it well when he wrote, "There is no reality more breathtaking than Jesus Christ. He is not safe, but He is stunning."[2]

Recently, my wife Gerrie and I were part of a small group that met on Sunday afternoons in the home of one of the members of our church. The group consisted of about fourteen adults and a few children. We gathered together each week for a time of sharing God's Word, praying, and encouraging one another. One week, God gave us the gift of His very presence. We experienced the revelation of His tender nearness. Liz Willson, one of the women in our group, describes the experience:

One Sunday afternoon, we were considering the love of God as expressed in both Ephesians 3:14–21 and 1 Corinthians 13. While we were reflecting on these passages, He broke in on us. As we considered that He is love, He, in expression of that great love, made His presence known to us. There was a great stillness and, for me, an incredible awareness of His holiness. No one moved, not even the children. No one spoke. We were effectively mute before such a One. The room was utterly quiet—so much so that even breathing seemed intrusive. For a full fifteen minutes we sat in His presence that way, worshiping Him in silence.

In those fifteen minutes, the Holy Spirit lingered around us and breathed upon us. He let us glimpse Jesus Christ with our inner souls. We knew that we were in God's holy and loving presence. Our souls, laid bare before Him, were overcome with His holiness, His purity, and His love. His nearness *is* stunning.

A Distinguishing Presence

Moses says in Exodus 33:16 that God's presence distinguishes God's people from all the other people of the earth. God's people are set apart from the world to be His holy ones (1 Peter 1:13–16). Instead of worshiping idols, they worship the true and living God (Exodus 20:3–4). Instead of living unrighteously, they diligently seek to do what is right and pleasing in God's sight (Ephesians 5:3–12). Instead of seeking self, they pursue lives of sacrificial love for one another (John 13:34–35). In place of being filled with works of the flesh (Galatians 5:19–21), they are filled with the fruit of His Spirit (Galatians 5:22–23). They submit to one another, and live in harmony so that God can command His blessing to be with them (Psalm 133). The oil upon the head and flowing down spoken about in this Psalm is none other than the Holy Spirit who reveals God's presence.

One of the reasons Jesus asked His Father to send this "other Helper" like Himself was so we could experience and enjoy the presence of Jesus here and now, and be conformed to His likeness. This is also why we need to ask, and keep on asking, for His presence as our Lord taught us (Luke 11:13). The Psalmist wrote, "Seek the Lord and his strength; seek his presence continually" (Psalm 105:4 ESV). Isaiah 55:6 commands us, "Seek the LORD while He may be found; call upon Him while He is near." Of course, asking must be done with faith as Mark 11:24 instructs us, "All things for which you pray and ask, believe that you have received them, and they will be granted you." We ask believing that our Father will faithfully answer because He promised and cannot lie. As our perfect, loving heavenly Father, He is ready to hear and answer. If, because of His love, He gave Jesus to die for us when we were His enemies, how much more now that we are His children will He give to us the reality of Jesus' presence? He happily does so.

Dr. A. B. Simpson, founder of the missionary denomination, The Christian and Missionary Alliance, writes about the "behind-the-scenes" work of the Holy Spirit:

> The great business of the Holy Spirit is to stand behind the scenes and make Jesus real. Just as the telescope reveals not itself, but the stars beyond, so Christ is revealed by the Holy Spirit, as the medium of our spiritual vision . . . Through the telephone of prayer, we may catch the very voice of our absent Master and be conscious of the heart-throbs of His love . . . The presence of the Comforter but makes Him nearer and dearer, and enables us to realize and know that we are in Him and He in us . . . The result of that interior revelation of Christ meant for Paul a deepened sense of the presence of Christ, "intimately, ravishingly near."[3]

This "ravishing" and "intimate" presence of Christ changes our lives, and with His authentic revealed presence within us, we are distinguished and separate from all other peoples in the world.

A Disturbing Analysis

Michael Yaconelli in his book, *Dangerous Wonder*, wrote, "The most critical issue facing Christians is not abortion, pornography, the disintegration of the family, moral absolutes . . . drugs, racism, sexuality . . . THE CRITICAL ISSUE TODAY IS DULLNESS. We have lost our astonishment. The Good News is no longer good news; it is okay news. Christianity is no longer life *changing*; it is life *enhancing*. Jesus doesn't change people into wild-eyed radicals any more, He changes them into 'nice people.'"[4]

If we belong to a reigning, ever-present, all-powerful Lord, who possesses all authority in heaven and on earth, then should we not expect to see Him do what would cause us to have, in the words of A. W. Tozer, "astonished reverence"? Should we not experience, again in Tozer's words, "admiration to the point of wonder and delight"? Should we not be renewed again and again by glimpses of His glory with us?

Too seldom do we know the manifest presence of Jesus in our churches. Sunday after Sunday we go through the motions. We sing, pray, preach, receive an offering, and go home without the real and powerful manifest presence of Jesus. We take the comfortable position that Jesus promised His presence, so He must be here. Indeed He is present by His omnipresence, but there is a vast difference between His omnipresence and when He steps into our very midst through the veil that hides Him. When this happens we realize and sense deeply within our souls, *God is here*! We are moved to the core of our beings. It is an indescribable encounter!

We often casually claim His presence by faith but do not actually expect anything much different to happen than what we have always known. Our prayers are often nothing more than wishful thinking rather than heartfelt thirsting after God. We pray our usual prayers but do not specifically trust God to keep His promises. We play childish games of "let's pretend all is well" when the truth is we are sickly, anemic, and powerless. We speak the language of the Spirit without the reality of genuine experience. Often lost people who come into our services are not struck by the presence of God but rather they encounter routine and dull religion (1 Corinthians

14:24–25). There may be enthusiastic singing and good preaching and a well-orchestrated service, but God's profound presence is missing.

J. I. Packer wrote: "The New Testament has a phrase for the failure in question: We may, it says, *quench* the Spirit by resisting or undervaluing his work, and by declining to yield to his influence (*see* Acts 7:51; Hebrews 10:29). The picture is of putting out a fire by pouring water on it." He points out that the Spirit can be quenched both personally and corporately. Then Dr. Packer makes a very disturbing observation that urgently warns us:

> It should be noted, too, that while one may effectively put out a fire by dousing it, one cannot make it burn again simply by stopping pouring water; it has to be lighted afresh. Similarly, when the Spirit has been quenched, it is beyond our power to undo the damage we have done; we can only cry to God in penitence, asking that he will revive his work.
>
> Now it is hard to deny that we inherit today a situation in which the Spirit of God has been quenched. Unnatural as it may be, the Spirit's power is absent from the majority of our churches. What has caused that? In some quarters, certainly, it is the direct result of devaluing the Bible, and the gospel and wandering out of the green pastures of God's Word into the barren flats of human speculation. In other places, however, where the 'old paths' of evangelical belief have not been abandoned, the quenching of the Spirit is due to attitudes, and inhibitions on the personal and practical level, which have simply stifled his work.[5]

Often the Spirit is quenched because of pride, fear, doubt, and toleration of known sin. We are afraid of what will happen if we do not maintain strict control, and therefore we do not allow the Spirit to have His way. We doubt that God wants to do anything different than what we have known for so long. In fact, many have never seen a real moving of God's Spirit and have little expectation of anything changing. We are too proud to admit that something is lacking and that most of what we do in church can be explained in terms of our own human effort. Because of our low view of God's holiness we have a low view of the seriousness of sin. Therefore, sin is excused in our lives and the lives of fellow believers in our churches. We are much like the church at Laodicea who thought they were rich, and had become wealthy, and had need of nothing, and yet did not know that God saw them as wretched and miserable and poor and blind and naked (Revelation 3:14–22). If we have money for our ministries, a good attendance, a sense of excitement, and good praise times that make us feel good, then we quell our consciences by saying, "God is blessing us."

Israel wandered around in the desert for forty years because of unbelief and disobedience, and yet they were still blessed by God. However, the blessing they experienced was minimal compared to what He wanted to pour out upon them. Is God's blessing to us minimal or is it His blessing in fullness? We urgently need the Lord to show us in our hearts the true condition of our individual lives and our churches as He sees us. Then, if we yearn for Him to be glorified—truly want His honor above all else—we will cry out to Him until the Fire of heaven lights the fire we have carelessly extinguished.

Conditions for His Revealed Presence

Jesus promises to disclose Himself to His obedient ones (John 14:21), and obviously, disobedience prevents this from happening. If you ignore, tolerate, or excuse known sin in your life, are you an obedient one? If you are not wholly available to Jesus Christ to do whatever He wills, are you an obedient one? If you are not walking in faith, depending on Him for all things, are you an obedient one? Unforgiveness and resentment in your heart are not obedience. Immorality and sensuality in your life are not obedience. Selfishness and insistence on your own way are not obedience. Failure to love and seek God with your whole heart is not obedience. Dishonesty and deceit are not obedience. Pride and arrogance are not obedience. Lying and cheating are not obedience. Sin grieves the Holy Spirit, and self-rule quenches Him. Could this be the reason why many

Christians do not know how deeply God loves them, and few rarely experience, if ever, His holy presence? Is unholiness the reason Jesus does not come near many churches' worship services? Is prayer in vain when sin is tolerated instead of the pursuit of holiness before the Lord? Is the blessing missed that God longs to give His people because He looks upon the sinful condition of their hearts and is grieved. In the June 26th entry in *Morning and Evening*, Charles Spurgeon says, "An unholy church! It is useless to the world, and of no esteem among men. It is an abomination, hell's laughter, heaven's abhorrence."[6] God instructs us, "Who may ascend into the hill of the LORD? / And who may stand in His holy place? / He who has clean hands and a pure heart, / Who has not lifted up his soul to falsehood / And has not sworn deceitfully. He shall receive a blessing from the LORD and righteousness from the God of his salvation" (Psalm 24:3–5).

Humbling Ourselves

James 4:8 contains both a command and a promise concerning God's nearness. He wrote to the first-century Christians, "Draw near to God and He will draw near to you. Cleanse your hands, you sinners and purify your hearts, you double-minded." He then proceeds to speak of true repentance and humility before the Lord (James 4:9– 10). It is so simple, a condition followed by a promise. His nearness makes you conscious of what you are, and what you are not, before a holy One like Him. Known sin in your life must then be confessed. The only way to find relief is by humbly repenting before the Lord followed by receiving forgiveness from Him. Honest confession with repentance before the Lord humbles us, and prayerful longing above all else for Him to be honored and glorified prepares the way for the Spirit's sovereign work.

I heard Henry Blackaby, a former Baptist pastor of a congregation in Canada and now an internationally known author, say on a taped message just this week that whenever their church went for a time without sensing the manifest presence of God, they would stop and seek Him about what the sin might be that hindered Him from being manifestly present among them. Most churches, however, try to fix any perceived problem with some fleshly effort, like a new program, a new emphasis, a new project, or a new format. Some even fire the pastor thinking that a new one will bring fresh life to the church. Anything and everything will be tried instead of humbly seeking the face of God with repentance until heaven answers and the Spirit breathes upon them.

When the way has been prepared for the Lord, then the Spirit will reveal the magnificent presence of Jesus at selected moments by His sovereign choice. Between those times, we seek to please Him by our persistent faith and obedience. We enjoy the Lord's promised presence day to day by quiet, resting faith, but always we should thirst for more of Him and long to have glimpses of His presence revealed. We should tend our hearts and our lives so that we are ready at any moment for Him to reveal His presence. Like the bride in The Song of Solomon who longs to be near her lover, our souls should say, "I must seek him whom my soul loves" (Song of Solomon 3:1, 2). She sought him until she found him.

Because of a unique experience I had as a conference speaker years ago, I can say along with Spurgeon that indeed an unholy church is useless to the world. I was not prepared for what God chose to do for me during those days. I share the story below as a testimony of God's revealed presence to me regarding His holiness and its place in the church.

In the early 1970s, I was invited with some other men to speak at a conference on revival in California. The other men were older than I and were well-known, more experienced Bible teachers. I went with a strong sense of inferiority and inadequacy. I was scheduled to speak on the Christian's authority in Christ. As I traveled by plane across our country, I had a growing burden inside. In the afternoon on the day of my arrival, we had a team prayer meeting. We gathered at the front of the auditorium where the conference would take place, got down before the Lord, and began to pray. Only after the others had prayed did I have a release to pray. When I began to pray, what came forth was a new burden that I had never expressed before: God wants a holy people. My prayers poured forth from deep inside with passion and feeling. The prayer meeting ended and the conference coordinator said to me, "Perhaps you are supposed to preach on holiness." There was only one problem—I had not prepared any messages on holiness. As a pastor in his early thirties, I had never spoken on holiness, and the conference was scheduled to begin the next morning. My first sermon was scheduled fairly early in the conference schedule, and then later I was to speak three more times.

After supper that evening, I went back to my motel room and went to bed early still planning to speak on our authority in Christ. The next morning I awoke early, quite a bit before daybreak. The weight of my assignment was heavy upon me. I got up and knelt down by my bed to pray. As I prayed, the same burden expressed the afternoon before began to flow forth. Suddenly, without any anticipation of such a thing, the Lord was present. I knew I was in the presence of Holy God. It was unlike anything I had experienced before. His purity and His holiness were stunning and almost overwhelming. His complete knowledge of me, but without condemnation, caused me to weep and repent for being a sinful man. I felt like a worm and would have crawled under the carpet if possible. I knew what Peter felt in Luke 5:8 when he said, "Go away from me Lord, for I am a sinful man!" My whole being was impacted by this heart revelation from my holy Lord. I was at His feet and engulfed by His presence where no words were adequate to express my soul and only my tears provided limited relief. That surprise encounter has affected me to this day.

After a while, I rose from my knees. Immediately, four messages came to me with Scriptures and outlines. I grabbed my pen and began making notes. Quickly the messages took shape on the pages, and soon I had four sermons on holiness. The response of the hearers over the next days indicated that God had indeed spoken. I had never had this experience before, nor have I had it since—that experience of having God change a series of messages so clearly, swiftly, and particularly as He dictated by His Spirit for His purposes.

Seeking and Finding Him

Our focus must be on seeking God and not emotional, religious experiences. Even pagan worshipers have religious experiences, but the true God certainly is not the author of those experiences. However, for those who seek Him with all their heart, God delights to give these surprise gifts of Christ's revealed nearness. Jesus discloses Himself by the Holy Spirit to the eyes of our hearts and to the inner sensing of our spirits. The sight is most beautiful and humbling to behold. The inner experience is beyond any other human experience on earth.

Our responsibility is to seek Him through persistent prayer, consistent meditation on His Word, true worship from the heart, and even fasting. He rewards those who diligently seek Him. Scripture does not provide a formula with steps to follow in order to guarantee the revelation of Christ's presence. Our responsibility is to hunger and thirst for Him and His righteousness. He promises emphatically to satisfy those who long for Him. We find it easier to long for success in ministry instead of Him, or happiness instead of Him, or deliverance from difficult circumstances instead of Him, or His blessing instead of Him, or some emotional experience instead of Him. He reserves Himself for the one who longs for Him and Him only—the beloved who desires the Lover and His nearness.

Mike DiMaria is a pastor who worked with youth and young adults at New Covenant Baptist Church in Denham Springs, Louisiana. As a seasoned youth worker, he was conducting a camp one summer during which time he had a personal experience of Christ choosing to draw near and reveal His astonishing presence. As you will read below, Mike was not spending those days and moments seeking an emotional encounter with Jesus:

> My surprise visit from Christ through His Holy Spirit began at a kids' camp one summer when Eric Ball was our guest speaker. For the entire week he spoke about the love of God. As a pastor for the past ten years and a veteran of ministry for over twenty years, God's love is a concept that I'm familiar with. To be honest I was a little upset that we were paying Eric all this money to speak, and all he kept preaching was how much God loves us. What I've found in this life is that often we become indifferent to those things that should mean the most to us.
>
> God touched my life with a fresh renewing of just how much He loves me after camp was over.

The Sunday following the end of camp, during the youth group's prayer and praise time, I simply asked the Lord to remind me just how much He really did love me. In the next moment, God stepped out of heaven, wrapped His arms around me, and began to love me in a way that I had never known. It was a physical, emotional, and spiritual experience. I liken it to taking a hot shower on a bone-chilling January day. His love just seemed to pour out on top of my head and run over me to the bottom of my toes. I was melted to my seat and, for the longest time, could not move and did not want to move. I simply wanted to enjoy this great gift of His presence in my life at that moment. I thank Him for letting me experience Him in a new and fresh way that day.

The fullness of God's blessing through the fullness of God's Spirit living and working in and through our lives is available for every Christian. Enjoyment of Christ's nearness is possible for every believer—*without exception*! So while we are not to seek after what Oswald Chambers called "exceptional moments of inspiration," we are to desire God and pursue Him with the expectancy that He is eager to grant to us the pleasure of His companionship, His nearness, and His fullness to be evidence of His presence in our lives.

Jonathan Goforth, a missionary to China in the early nineteen hundreds who experienced an outpouring of the Spirit where he served, wrote in his book, *By My Spirit*, "We are convinced that the majority of Christian people are living on a plane far below what our Master planned for them."[7] Andrew Murray, who was a pastor in South Africa around the same time, wrote: "God wills a great deal of blessing to His people which never comes to them. He wills it most earnestly, but they do not will it, and it cannot come to them."[8] Psalm 91:1 says, "He who dwells in the shelter of the Most High / Will abide in the shadow of the Almighty." Charles Haddon Spurgeon, the great preacher of England in the late 1800s, commented on this verse in his book, *The Treasury of David*:

The blessings here promised are not for all believers, but for those who live in close fellowship with God. Every child of God looks towards the inner sanctuary and the mercy-seat, yet all do not dwell in the most holy place; they run to it at times and enjoy occasional approaches, but they do not habitually reside in the mysterious presence. Those who through rich grace obtain unusual and continuous communion with God, so as to abide in Christ and Christ in them, become possessors of rare and special benefits, which are missed by those who follow afar off, and grieve the Holy Spirit of God.[9]

I have a wonderful story to share about a man I met several years ago whose life exemplifies what Goforth, Murray, and Spurgeon speak about—this man seeks to live on the highest plane His Master intends. He anticipates and receives the great deal of blessing God wills to him, and he is a possessor of those rare and special benefits which come to those in continuous communion with God. A few years ago I went to speak at a church in California. The pastor who was arranging the series of meetings told me that the music would be provided by a man named Sylvester Blue, a man that he believed had the most beautiful voice he had ever heard. Sylvester and his family came and sang before I brought the message. As he sang, God's presence was revealed in that place—a presence both wonderful and humbling. Gerrie, my wife, is not a very outwardly emotional person, but she needed to put her hand over her mouth because she thought she was going to weep out loud. She could only close her eyes, while in her heart she longed to get down on her face and only worship the Lord.

After the service was over, Sylvester and I began to talk together. One of the first things he said was, "The most important thing is the presence of God." I almost fell over. No one else had ever spoken to me about that. This truth that had been so central to my personal journey, and now was so central in my thoughts and prayers, was being spoken to me by a complete stranger. He continued speaking, "Jerry, it is not the voice," and he pointed with his fingers to his throat. "Many men can sing. It is the presence of God that is most important. After midnight whenever God wakes me up, I get up and pray. I ask God for His presence." Later I invited this wonderful family to our church to minister to us. The same thing occurred; as Sylvester sang, the presence of God came upon us.

Assurances of His Nearness

Sometimes the revealed presence of Jesus Christ by His Spirit can be so felt that it affects your physical being. His presence brushes against you. His hand is upon you. A revelation of Him passes right through your soul. You know that the King of Heaven has come and visited you and you feel the lingering embrace of this Holy Being whom you cannot see.

During these times, conviction of sin and failure is accompanied by a profoundly deep awareness of being loved by this Holy One from heaven. A window of heaven opens and a measure of its rarified atmosphere falls upon earth in a particular place at a particular time yielding moments that are indescribable, unexplainable, and unforgettable. And you respond to the Holy One of heaven with a hushed reverence, a sober humility, and a more pure worship.

Sometimes stunned silence is the only appropriate response. At other times "joy inexpressible . . . full of glory" is one's experience (1 Peter 1:8). In either case, we become aware that we are finite, created beings who have been visited by an infinite, invisible, and eternal Creator, Redeemer, and exalted Lord. The sovereign God who is always present everywhere has drawn inexplicably and breathtakingly near in the Person of Jesus Christ by His Spirit.

Charles Spurgeon writes lucidly about John 14:21, the portion of the Upper Room discourse where Jesus promises to reveal Himself to those disciples who love and obey Him:

> The Lord Jesus gives special revelations of Himself
> to his people. Even if Scripture did not declare this,
> there are many of the children of God who could
> testify the truth of it from their own experience. They
> have had manifestations of their Lord and Saviour

Jesus Christ in a peculiar manner, such as no mere reading or hearing could afford. In the biographies of eminent saints, you will find many instances recorded in which Jesus has been pleased, in a very special manner to speak to their souls, and to unfold the wonders of His person; yea, so have their souls been steeped in happiness that they have thought themselves to be in heaven, whereas they were not there, though they were well nigh on the threshold of it—for when Jesus manifests Himself to his people, it is heaven on earth; it is paradise in embryo; it is bliss begun. Especial manifestations of Christ exercise a holy influence on the believer's heart . . . Thus there will be three effects of nearness to Jesus—humility, happiness, and holiness. May God give them to thee, Christian.[10]

Spurgeon is correct when he says, "There are many of the children of God who could testify the truth of [special revelations] from their own experience." Dwight L. Moody, Jonathan Edwards, George Whitefield, Charles G. Finney, Blaise Pascal, and a multitude of others have given testimony to such experiences. Thomas Aquinas, a theologian and prolific writer of the medieval church, spoke of a time when the glory of God brushed by him. Brennan Manning tells about it: "The story goes that Thomas Aquinas, perhaps the world's greatest theologian, toward the end of his life suddenly stopped writing. When his secretary complained that his work was unfinished, Thomas replied: 'Brother Reginald, when I was at prayer a few months ago, I experienced something of the reality of Jesus Christ. That day, I lost all appetite for writing. In fact, all I have ever written about Christ seems now to me to be like straw.'"[11]

Another saint who could testify to the "sweet delight" of Christ's presence was Sarah Pierrepoint Edwards, the wife of the great American theologian Jonathan Edwards (1703–1758). Sarah was converted to Christ at age five. When Jonathan was only eighteen and Sarah was thirteen, he wrote about her:

They say there is a young lady in [New Haven] who is beloved of that almighty Being, who made and rules the world, and that there are certain seasons in which this great Being, in some way or other invisible, comes to her and fills her mind with exceeding sweet delight, and that she hardly cares for anything, except to meditate on him—that she expects after a while to be received up where he is, to be raised up out of the world and caught up into heaven; being assured that he loves her too well to let her remain at a distance from him always. There she is to dwell with him, and to be ravished with his love and delight forever. Therefore, if you present all the world before her, with the richest of its treasures, she disregards it and cares not for it, and is unmindful of any pain or affliction. She has a strange sweetness in her mind, and singular purity in her affections; is most just and conscientious in all her actions; and you could not persuade her to do anything wrong or sinful, if you would give her all the world, lest she should offend this great Being. She is of a wonderful sweetness, calmness and universal benevolence of mind; especially after those seasons in which this great God has manifested himself to her mind. She will sometimes go about from place to place, singing sweetly; and seems to be always full of joy and pleasure; and no one knows for what. She loves to be alone, and to wander in the fields and on the mountains, and seems to have someone invisible always conversing with her.[12]

Sarah Edwards as a wife and mother continued her close walk with God. On her thirty-second birthday she wrote in her diary:

I felt very uneasy and unhappy at my being so low in grace. I thought I very much needed help from God, and found a spirit of earnestness to seek help from Him, that I might have more holiness. When

I had been for a time earnestly wrestling with God
for it, I felt within myself great quietness of spirit,
unusual submission to God, and great willingness to
wait upon Him with respect to the time and manner
in which He should help me; and wished that He
should take His own time and His own way to do it.
I cannot find words to express how certain the love
of God appeared to me. My safety and happiness,
eternal enjoyment of God's immutable love, seemed
as durable and unchangeable as God Himself. Melted
and overcome by the sweetness of this assurance, I
fell into a great flow of tears, and could not forbear
weeping aloud . . . These words seemed to come over
and over in my mind; "My God, my all; My God, my
all." The presence of God was so near and so real that
I seemed scarce conscious of anything else.[13]

The felt nearness of God's presence is not reserved for great
theologians and great preachers. His revealed presence is available
for all who know Him. This presence can be distinguished even by
a child. I was speaking at a summer conference in Greenville, South
Carolina one summer and a young boy about twelve named Zachary
was attending with his parents. This conference was one of those
times when God's Spirit came down in a unique way that made the
presence of Christ so real. Young Zachary needed no prompting
about what he experienced. He shared freely with his neighbor, his
great-grandmother, and his parents what he experienced. "There was
such an overwhelming sense of the presence of God that I thought
God was going to come right into the room. I thought Jesus Himself
was going to walk right in the door. I couldn't stay in my chair and
I couldn't stand up. I had to get down on my knees." So whether
one is great or small, known or unknown in this world, when Jesus
comes close to us and His presence is revealed to us, we all can
testify together that His nearness is real. And it humbles us!

God wants you to be near Him. God wants you to seek Him with
your whole heart. God wants you to know His nearness and at times
experience His presence as if He has physically brushed against you

or even embraced you. Knowing what it will do for you He says we should "seek His face [presence] continually" (Psalm 105:4).

This is His best gift—Himself. This is our supreme blessing—Himself revealed to us and so near to us that inwardly we do catch glimpses of His glory. These moments when heaven kisses earth—where we live—can never be forgotten.

Dear gracious, loving Father,

I cannot comprehend that You would give Yourself to me. I cannot fathom that You, so holy and pure, would draw near me. Even in all eternity I will not be able to understand that You love me in spite of my sin, desire to be with me, and want me to see You in all the beauty of Your glory. I am deeply grateful that I can enjoy Your presence every day through simple, childlike faith. I praise You that You want to give me special times when You surprise me with heavenly gifts of Your presence. Father, how I need You in all that You are. How my church needs You and the holy breath of Your presence upon us. Please be merciful and lead us to long for You and be satisfied with nothing less than You. Give us a thirst for You that will compel us to seek You and crave Your presence near us. I ask this for Your pleasure and Your glory. Amen.

Notes

[1] David Hazard, *Majestic Is Your Name*, (Minneapolis, Minnesota: Bethany House Publishers, 1993), 13.

[2] John Piper, *The Dangerous Duty of Delight*, (Sisters, Oregon: Multnomah Publishers, 2001), 8.

[3] Words of A. B. Simpson, quoted by J. Oswald Sanders, *Enjoying Intimacy with God*, (Grand Rapids, Michigan: Discovery House Publishers, 2000), 74–75.

[4] Michael Yaconelli, *Dangerous Wonder*, (Colorado Springs, Colorado: NavPress, 1998), 23.

[5] Packer, *Keep in Step with the Spirit*, 252–253.

[6] Spurgeon, *Morning & Evening*, June 26, Evening reading.

[7] Jonathan Goforth, *By My Spirit*, (Minneapolis, Minnesota: Bethany Fellowship, Inc., 1942), 13.

[8] Source unknown.

[9] C. H. Spurgeon, *The Treasury of David*, (Byron Center, Michigan: Associated Publishers and Authors, Inc., 1970), Vol. II, 230.

[10] Spurgeon, *Morning & Evening*, May 12, Morning reading.

[11] Brennan Manning, *The Ragamuffin Gospel*, 199–200. According to *The New International Dictionary of the Christian Church*, Thomas Aquinas (1224–1274) was the greatest philosopher and theologian of the medieval church. He was born in Italy, studied in Paris and Cologne, and for most of his life taught in Paris. His influence on the Christian Church through his many writings has been enormous, although his unbiblical errors were repudiated at the Reformation.

[12] Words of Sarah Edwards quoted by Jonathan Edwards, *A Jonathan Edwards Reader*, Edited by John E. Smith, Harry S. Stout, and Kenneth P. Minkema, (New Haven and London: Yale University Press, 1995), 281.

[13] Source unknown.

CHAPTER NINE

The Power of Jesus' Presence

> *The New Testament writers expect that every*
> *Christian community will show forth the power of*
> *the Holy Spirit, for to enjoy a rich outpouring of*
> *the Holy Spirit is a privilege entailed upon the New*
> *Testament church as such. For churches to lack the*
> *Spirit's powerful working in their corporate life*
> *is by biblical standards unnatural, just as heresy*
> *is; and this unnatural state of affairs can only be*
> *accounted for in terms of human failure.*
> —J. I. Packer, *Keep in Step with the Spirit*

The presence of Christ revealed to us by the Holy Spirit is often attended with a manifestation of His mighty power accompanied by an acute awareness of His omnipotent character. During two of these remarkable experiences, I witnessed visible demonstrations of His power in control. In this chapter, others will share testimonies of what they saw God accomplish through obedient and yielded hearts.

In 1977 I spoke at a summer youth retreat in central Florida for a church from Georgia. In the early evening session after supper, I spoke for a very brief time. It was no more than ten to fifteen minutes, and then I sent the group out to spend time alone with the Lord. When they returned, I asked if anyone had something they would like to share. What followed was quite surprising and amazing. One person after another stood up, both students and adults, to confess sin and make commitments to the Lord. This continued for a long time. The Holy Spirit had come upon this group revealing the powerful presence of Jesus Christ in our midst.

Scott McHugh tells of that event. He was the associate pastor of the church in Lawrenceville, Georgia. Along with other responsibilities, he worked with the youth.

It was the summer of 1977 in Central Florida. Our youth group of about 60 students traveled to Lake George Assembly for a five-day retreat. Over the last two years the Lord had been moving mightily in Central Baptist, our church. Many students were hungry for a close walk with God, and as we prepared for this retreat, there was great anticipation of what God would do among us. We knew our invited speaking guest would have a Word from the Lord for us.

Our first sessions were without incident . . . without ANY incident. There was no movement of the Spirit. We had come anticipating God to bless mightily, but there was a blatant dryness in the meetings. God was calling us to pray and so, pray we did. We cried out to the Lord in desperate brokenness and pressed in to plead for His blessings on the retreat. We prayed for quite a while with a humble insistence asking that God break through all barriers to His blessings. After that time of intercession, the Holy Spirit released us with an assurance of His answer.

It is true that prayer is striking the winning blow and ministry is gathering the results.

The next day Jerry arrived. As he ministered the Word of God, those students' hearts began to melt under the conviction of the Holy Spirit. The power of God overshadowed that meeting and lives began to be transformed to His glory. It started when a student who was a leader among his peers stood in the middle of the meeting, broken and weeping with an overflow of confession of sin. He confessed his hypocrisy and lying. He confessed he was not what he appeared to be and his need of the Lord. Brokenness and godly sorrow spread over the whole room. Student after student would then stand to confess more deep sin. An atmospheric, urgent, godly sorrow gripped their hearts. As sin was confessed, these broken-hearted young people were freed from spiritual strongholds that had held them for years. One leader of the group stood and said that he had been a chronic liar and he was repentant over his hypocrisy. Another stood who was formerly the biggest drug dealer in the local high school. Only a few months before, he had given his life to Christ and was gloriously saved. Yet, there were areas in his life that he had not given to God. He (now a Christian musician) shared with amazing transparency and was sent out of the meeting by Jerry to be prayed for by some adult counselors. When he returned the power of God had set him free from a number of tormenting spirits such as drugs and lust and other things that I cannot remember. For hours, these students met with God as they humbled themselves before Him. Heaven did come down, and as the Scripture says, "They looked unto Him and were radiant and their faces shall never be ashamed."

This was one of the most vivid examples of God sending His Word . . . that I have ever seen. It was so powerful and was used by God to shape their lives to this day. The memories of those days have remained fresh all these years, and I have had the privilege of telling this testimony over and over again to various audiences and witness them marvel at the faithful grace and awesome power of our Lord Jesus Christ.

As a result of this retreat, the youth and their leaders began to be concerned and to pray for the adults in their church. Some months later Pastor Glenn Shepherd invited me to come for a series of meetings. One night after a message on the sixth chapter of Romans, I called for Pastor Shepherd to come and pray for his congregation. He came to the pulpit and with deep conviction he leaned over the pulpit to pray. With tears he poured out his heart to God. After he finished praying, he looked at me and said, "Jerry, do you have anything else?" I said, "No." He turned back to face the congregation and dismissed them and then sat down on a chair on the other side of the platform. I had never seen what followed in a Baptist church before, and I had been in many. No one moved. The congregation just sat and stared straight ahead. Two or three in the back got up and left. The rest continued to sit and look straight ahead as if quite stunned. I was bewildered as to what to do. I went to the pulpit and asked if anyone wanted to give a testimony. A young man came up to speak, but the words hung in his throat like he was choking on a bone. Again and again, he opened his mouth to speak only to make a guttural sound like he was choking. I realized he had a problem and sent him out with Scott and the pastor. The people continued to sit and stare in stunned silence. Finally, I went to find the pastor who was seeking to help the young man in a room behind the auditorium, and said, "Pastor, your people need you. They are still just sitting there in silence. I will stay here and minister to him." I was bewildered by it all. What do you do at a time like this? I had never been at a place like this before.

So I walked across the room away from where Scott and the young man were seated while asking the Lord what to do. Just as I got to the other side of the room, suddenly the Lord gave me a strong, clear impression as to the man's problem. I turned and confronted him, "What is the immorality in your life?" He knew the Lord had revealed it to him and was pierced by my question. With repentance he confessed his sin to the Lord. We prayed for him, and the Lord instantly set him free. We then returned to the auditorium where the pastor was presiding and the congregation was singing and giving testimony. The young man who had just been set free by the Lord through the Holy Spirit went to the pulpit and confessed that what he was planning to say earlier was not true, and the Lord would not let him say it. He then told us how God had met him. With his newfound freedom he grew in Christ and later went on to serve as a missionary.

Another young man, Mike Griffin, was attending the meetings because he lived in the Atlanta, Georgia area not far from the church and had a deep hunger for God. Mike is now Associate Pastor at First Baptist Church, Lilburn, Georgia with many years of fruitful ministry. He writes what he witnessed during those meetings:

> As a teenager in the 1970s, I had the privilege of being an eyewitness to several special manifestations of God's holy presence in what I would consider to be a God-sent revival. One of those special times was at Central Baptist Church in Lawrenceville, Georgia. By God's sovereign providence and by the work of the Holy Spirit, the Lord God visited those meetings with a special demonstration of His holy presence and power. I can remember three distinct characteristics of that manifestation of God's presence.
>
> First, there was a great sense of brokenness. I remember that when one of the services concluded there was such an awareness of the holiness of God that no one moved. We just sat there still unable to move. When some movement occurred, it was movement toward prostration. Grown men got on their faces and cried out in brokenness over their sin. The Holy Spirit effected a breaking up of the fallow ground, which brought a deep sense of conviction and humility as we were placed before the eternal spotlight of God's holiness. Because of our sin and apathy our hearts were broken before a holy God. The Holy Spirit brought a consuming desire to forsake all sin and abandon ourselves in obedience to the Lord Jesus Christ.
>
> Secondly, I can remember the demonstration of the power of God. As a result of those meetings, the

power of God brought the unsaved to faith in Christ. I remember one young man who was intensely hardened to the gospel. His life of sin and perversion made him among the most difficult to hear the truth of the gospel. He was brought from death to life in Christ as a result of those meetings. This was "the power of God unto salvation" displayed. I remember watching in amazement as I witnessed miraculous healing for the first time. The pastor's wife gave testimony just moments after she was instantaneously healed of an encumbering physical difficulty. I can also remember the testimony about those who were delivered from demonic influence. As God demonstrated His power in healing and deliverance, there was also testimony from those who were set free from years of spiritual defeat

The third characteristic that I remember from this special manifestation of God's presence is that fruit "HAS" remained. I still have close relationships with several who attended those meetings. Several are serving the Lord in Christian ministry and others are faithfully serving Him in their local church where they attend. They are walking in the fullness of the Holy Spirit and are living in obedience to the Word of God. For many of them, the hunger for God and the passion for His glory have not waned, but only increased. The longing for God to manifest His presence again is represented by the cry of the Psalmist in Psalm 85:6, "Will You not revive us again, that Your people may rejoice in You?"

The Spirit's Power in Revival

The Holy Spirit can reveal the presence of Jesus in many ways. Much of the time these revelations may not be as dramatic as told above, but they are just as real. And then sometimes the revelations of His outpouring and presence are much bigger and more dramatic than I have ever seen in what is known as true revival. Throughout Christian history there have been great outpourings of the Holy Spirit over whole regions in various countries, both in the global east and west, and many books have been written documenting these miraculous events. Dr. Martyn Lloyd-Jones, the much-respected English pastor of the last century wrote in his classic book, *Revival*:

> The essence of a revival is that the Holy Spirit comes down upon a number of people together, upon a whole church, upon a number of churches, districts, or perhaps a whole country. That is what is meant by revival. It is, if you like, a visitation of the Holy Spirit, or another term that has often been used is this—an outpouring of the Holy Spirit. And the terms are interesting because you see what the people are conscious of is that it is as if something has suddenly come down upon them. The Spirit of God has descended into their midst, God has come down and is amongst them. A baptism, an outpouring, a visitation. And the effect of that is that they immediately become aware of his presence and of his power in a manner that they have never known before. I am talking about Christian people, about church members gathering together as they have done so many times before. Suddenly they are aware of his presence, they are aware of the majesty and the awe of God. The Holy Spirit literally seems to be presiding over the meeting and taking charge of it, and manifesting his power and guiding them, and leading them, and directing them. This is the essence of revival.[1]

This kind of outpouring of the Holy Spirit occurred in 1949 on the island of Lewis-and-Harris, one of the Outer Hebrides Islands off the northwest coast of Scotland. An urgent request came from praying people in the village of Barvas for Duncan Campbell to go there. Within a few weeks, Reverend Campbell went to the village of Barvas. Mr. P. S. Bristow shares about what happened in the foreword of a little book by Duncan Campbell, *The Price and Power of Revival*:

> Whole communities were mightily moved as "God came," and the following instance is typical of the scenes witnessed in the churches and in the homes of the people throughout the island: " . . . a crowded church, the service is over, the congregation reluctant to disperse stands outside the church in a silence that is tense. Suddenly a cry is heard within; a young man, burdened for the souls of his fellow men, is pouring out his soul in intercession. He prays until he falls into a trance and lies prostrate on the floor of the church. But Heaven has heard and the congregation, moved by the power of God, comes back into the church, and a wave of conviction sweeps over the gathering, moving strong men to cry for mercy. This service continued until the small hours of the morning, but so great was the distress and so deep the hunger which gripped men and women that they refused to go home though others were already assembling in another part of the parish; and a number of those who now made their way to the church were moved by a power they had not before experienced. Others were deeply convicted of sin and crying for mercy in their own homes before coming near the church. None who were present at this early morning visitation will forget the moving scenes—some weeping in sorrow and distress, others with joy and love filling their hearts, falling upon their knees, conscious only of the presence and power of God who had come in revival blessing. Within a matter of days the whole parish was in the grip of a spiritual awakening. Churches became crowded, with services continuing until three o'clock in the morning. Work was largely put aside as young and old were made to face eternal realities."[2]

I heard a man speak many years ago who was present during this mighty outpouring of God's Spirit. As a boy he had been paralyzed in his legs from polio and was unable to walk. As a grown man he was on his bed at home with his paralysis when God's presence suddenly came into the room. He knew the Lord had come and was instantly healed, got out of bed, and walked.

In his book, *Revival! A People Saturated with God*, Brian Edwards records the words of Joseph Kemp concerning how God worked powerfully at Charlotte Chapel in Edinburgh, Scotland in 1905. "There was nothing, humanly speaking, to account for what happened. Quite suddenly, upon one and another came an overwhelming sense of the reality and awfulness of His presence and of eternal things. Life, death, and eternity seemed suddenly laid bare."[3]

Edwards also indicates seven characteristics evident when God pours out His Spirit on a church:

- A renewed hunger for the Word of God
- A new earnestness and enthusiasm for prayer
- A passionate burden and concern for the lost
- An eclipse of time; people forget the clock but are not irresponsible
- A spirit of reconciliation; people forget minor differences
- A profound change in lives; even children demonstrate spiritual maturity[4]

The Spirit's Presence and Power Without Revival

Philip Yancey, a well-known American author of several books, poignantly wrote in his book, *The Jesus I Never Knew*, "Two words one could never think of applying to the Jesus of the Gospels: boring and predictable. How is it, then, that the church has tamed such a character—has, in Dorothy Sayer's words, 'very efficiently pared the claws of the Lion of Judah, certified Him as a fitting household pet for curates and pious old ladies'?"[5] If that is true of Jesus, then it is true of His Spirit. Worship services without Christ present are boring and predictable. They are planned, calculated, controlled, and executed by very sincere leaders but seldom are there surprises. Too infrequently does one sense that heaven has burst in upon a worship service. Too seldom do individual Christians have testimonies of having met the living and present Christ in a new, deep, and fresh way. When Jesus fills His people and His Church with Himself, it is not boring and it cannot be predicted. One never knows who He is going to touch next, or who He will use next, or when His presence will be revealed in a stunning way. We should live with expectancy like His first disciples. Surely they must have wondered, "What will He do next?" Every day was an adventure, every encounter an opportunity. He made their lives rich and full by His presence and with His unpredictable and unexplainable works. Why should it not be so for us now who are His disciples? He promised life abundant (John 10:10), life full of His peace (John 14:27), life full of His joy (John 15:11), life full of His Spirit (John 14:16–17) and His vitalizing presence with us always (Matthew 28:20). Oh yes, and tribulation as well (John 16:33).

I am speaking about Christ's revealed presence and active power among us even when there is not revival—a great outpouring of the Holy Spirit—as Dr. Lloyd-Jones defined it in the previous section on revival, and as it was illustrated by the account of revival in the Hebrides. Revival in that sense is larger, more intense, and sustained over a longer period of time, perhaps for weeks or months or even years. Christ's presence with power apart from revival should be a regular happening in our churches. And it can happen, will happen, if we are obedient and therefore spiritually healthy.

The Lord by His Spirit may come near in an overwhelming way or in a gentle way. His presence may be stunning or quietly perceptible. He gives Himself in Self-disclosure as is needed for the moment. He always keeps us aware that these times when He discloses His wonderful presence are by His sovereign choice. There are no formulas you can work to bring down such gifts. Heart preparation is necessary but nothing man does ever manipulates God to do anything. God responds to His children's humble and hungry hearts in His time, in His way. Glimpses of Him are His personal gifts for those who thirst for Him. He bestows these gifts whenever and however He chooses.

I told in Chapter 7 about speaking in a series of meetings in Greenville, South Carolina when the presence and power of Christ were revealed. This experience profoundly affected me and encouraged me regarding just what God wants to do in and for His churches. Through the years I have become convinced that what He looks for is humility, repentance where it is needful, hunger (thirst) expressed through prayer, and responsiveness to His Spirit.

Leona Morris, a dear faithful Christian sister, was also in those meetings. She recounts what happened:

> I remember the day the Holy Spirit visited our assembly at the Greenville Christian Fellowship (Greenville, South Carolina). The meeting had been preceded by about seven days with our guest speaker leading the services. At these meetings we were urged to allow the Holy Spirit to search our hearts to show us any lurking sin, confess, and repent of it and be done with it. This particular morning we assembled at 10:30 AM. The schedule was for us to adjourn at 12:00 noon.
>
> After the singing of hymns, our guest speaker began. There was heard quiet weeping by some, as the Holy Spirit was speaking to hearts. As the service proceeded there was more open weeping and confessions of sins by both young and old going forward to kneel before the Lord and crying out for cleansing. The youngest one I witnessed was about twelve years old. The oldest was in her eighties. (She had lived years thinking she was a Christian. She asked to be baptized and went on with the Lord giving praise for how good the Lord was to show her need to her.)
>
> The service continued, and there wasn't any more room near the altar to pray. People literally fell by their chairs to confess their sins and to beg for cleansing. There was no room to walk for a while

and no one seemed to want to. Only three or four left before the meeting adjourned at mid-afternoon. Even after dismissal people remained to give praise to God. What a joyous time!

I was in my very early forties then. I had never witnessed anything like it before or since, and this happened thirty years ago. It was such a manifest working of the Holy Spirit in yielded, obedient hearts.

Art Nuernberg, Executive Director for The Evangelical Institute of Greenville in South Carolina, was a college student then and was also present. He writes:

I was born again of the Spirit of God during a brief but powerful manifestation of the Lord's presence in the spring of 1972. Details of the work have faded over the thirty years but the deep impression of God's presence has not. Four definite memories of those days remain.

First, was the unexpected nature of what took place. The group that met together was both well taught and deeply committed to following the Lord. They had gathered out of a simple desire to study the Word together. It started as just another series of meetings, but as the week progressed there was an unusual and gradually deepening sense of the Lord in the midst.

Second, was the inescapable clarity of the messages given. The truths we heard were familiar. The style was not unusual. But the Spirit of God caught us in the spotlight of His scrutiny. I personally had been counting the cost of following the Lord for some time. Now compelling clarity urged me to move forward and corresponding conviction warned of the danger of delay.

Third, there was delivering power. I went forward at the end of one meeting seeking cleansing from guilt. I not only received cleansing but wonderful release from sin that had plagued me for years. The next day, plunged into the midst of temptation, I was profoundly aware of my new life and with it, new motivation and capacity to live God's way.

Finally, there was in the end the overwhelming sense of the joy of the Lord. Because of my college schedule I was not able to attend many of the meetings the second week. But one day I was so overwhelmed with gratitude and joy that I left classes and went to a remote spot on the campus not so much to pray as to pour out my heart through hymns to God. (This is hardly my style.) I could barely keep up with the flood of desire God had placed in my heart.

When God's Spirit has His way with a church like He did in the book of Acts, one cannot explain what happens. It is far beyond what man can accomplish. To be sure, God uses human instrumentality, but when the Breath of Heaven comes it cannot be explained or understood. Always it is shrouded in mystery. Always it glorifies God. Always it has a permanent effect upon those touched by it.

Several years ago a man began attending our church where I was pastor. His wife had been a faithful member for a long time. I watched him from Sunday to Sunday listen very attentively to the teaching of God's Word. On two or three Sundays he came to the front at an appropriate time and knelt down to pray. One Sunday he came after the worship service to talk with me. I prayed with him knowing that God was at work in his life. Here is his story in his own words:

Around the beginning of 1999, my life, when viewed from the outside seemed fine. I had a nice home, a beautiful wife, two lovely daughters, a job that provided me with plenty of money and plenty of free time. However, on the inside I could find no peace. I felt as though I was starting to unravel. This is when I started calling out to God, seeking Him, seeking truth. Inside I knew something had to be settled.

I did not realize it at the time but God heard my cries and had started me on an incredible journey. He brought into my life the people I needed to meet and led me to the places I needed to go.

After the worship service on September 26, 1999, I went to talk with the pastor. I told him I wanted to see God's face and hear His voice. He prayed for me and in that prayer he prayed for a filling of the Holy Spirit, and it happened. All I know is that I walked into that building one person and walked out another. I finally knew what it was to be born again. I was a new creation.

There is one more thing. Satan sets many snares, and over twenty years ago I had been caught in one. I had done drugs, even crack cocaine, and I was able to break free from all of them except marijuana. For many years I tried to free myself only to grow tired and give up. At the end of that prayer, Brother Jerry, without knowing my problem, prayed that if there was a hold on me that I become set free. Zap! It was finished. I was free. It was as though God had picked me up and taken me back to the day before I walked into that snare. The professionals of this world will say that what happened is impossible, but I say that with God all things are possible.

This is Jesus being Who He is, doing what He alone can do. The Holy Spirit ministered the presence of Jesus to this seeker that day and years later his heart is still aflame with love for Jesus.

I was in a southern state leading a church in a series of meetings. One day the associate pastor came to ask me if there was a time that we could talk. We set an appointment for the following afternoon. He came and began to speak, "What I am going to tell you no one else knows, not my pastor, not even my wife. When I was in the military before becoming a Christian, I watched pornogrophic films. I became a Christian and later entered the ministry, but I am still addicted to them. How can I be freed of this?" I replied, "If you will humble yourself by kneeling down before the Lord and ask Him, He will cleanse you and set you free." This brother with such heavy guilt and shame not only got on his knees but with desperation bent forward with his face almost touching the floor and with weeping asked the Lord Jesus to forgive him and set him free. The only way I know how to describe what happened is that Jesus' presence and power instantly set him free. I saw him during another visit to his area two years later. We encountered one another in a church parking lot and he came rushing over to me beaming with a smile and said, "Jerry, I have been free ever since."

I remember multitudes of happenings across the years just like the above, some even more dramatic. I have been wonder struck again and again as I witnessed Jesus step forth to make whole or set free or wash clean or make new or fill with His Spirit. We must not be afraid of the unexpected and unexplainable results that occur when Jesus comes near in His revealed presence with power. We cannot afford to react against wrong emphases some have made regarding the work of the Holy Spirit, and therefore be robbed of Christ's presence and power manifested among us. If the enemy interrupts with "strange fire," then the one presiding has the Lord's authority and the Spirit's guidance to handle it biblically and call it out of order. People are burdened today just like they were when He walked in the flesh. They are cast down, and in bondage, and bewildered, and confused, and full of guilt, and needy just as the people were two thousand years ago. Jesus has the same compassion today as He did then. He has the same power and authority now as then. He has given His Spirit—One just like Himself—to accomplish in and through us His works of love. The Holy Spirit has been given to be Christ with us here and now and to minister His presence and power through the Church as His body on earth. Preaching and teaching God's Word, as purely and accurately and clearly as possible, must have central place in a church's ministry. Doctrinal truth is foundational. Counseling has an important place for those who are in difficult places or have troubled souls. But there are situations where teaching, preaching, and counseling will not accomplish what must be done by Christ's power touching a life. His presence and power can be experienced among His people even when there is not a great outpouring of the Spirit in revival. This is why our heavenly Father poured out His Spirit profusely for all His children and churches. Can we ignore this and be satisfied with far less than our Father has given?

Thankfully, there *are* churches where the presence and power of Christ are evident. I know about the Brooklyn Tabernacle in Brooklyn, New York. This church demonstrates the truth of Christ's presence and power in "normal church life." I had read about the church in Pastor Cymbala's books and then visited them to see it firsthand for myself. There is no explanation for what happens there except the revealed presence and power of Jesus.[6] What is dreadfully sad to me is that this is so rare in our churches rather than being the norm that God intends for all churches.

Pursuing God in Prayer

The Bible clearly teaches that there are conditions when persistent prayer is required to obtain the blessing from God that we seek (Luke 11:5–13, 18:1–8). God wants us to pursue Him diligently, and in times of low spirituality, seek Him even desperately (Deuteronomy 4:29, Jeremiah 29:13, Hebrews 11:6). God is sickened when His church is lukewarm although they may feel like they are rich and have need of nothing (Revelation 3:14–17). It was to this church in Laodicea that Jesus said, "Behold, I stand at the door and knock" (Revelation 3:20). The appearance of success by worldly standards does not mean Christ is present with power. Even though this verse is often used for a salvation verse, the true meaning is that Jesus is standing at the door of His own church knocking to get back in because they have become satisfied *without* His presence. The church must recognize and reckon with its own spiritual poverty and open the door for Jesus to come in again with His powerful presence. When we become wholly dissatisfied with our lives and the condition of our churches then we will not, and cannot, be content with the way things have been. The Psalmist said, "My eyes shed streams of water, / Because they do not keep Your law" (Psalm 119:136).

Shakespeare wrote in his play, *Hamlet*, "Diseases desperate grown, by desperate appliance are reliev'd, or not at all."[7] When a church goes through its meetings without knowing the real and living presence of Jesus, it is in a state of desperate disease. We must become dissatisfied, even sick of the fact that we have let sin and selfishness and complacency and pride rob us of the God's richest blessing, which is none other than the presence and power of Jesus revealed by the Holy Spirit. We must humble ourselves and repent for the grievous act of quenching His Spirit.

Often our failure is because we do not thirst for Him. We think we have experienced the best there is, and yet all the time we have a haunting suspicion that there must be more than this. Is this the best of the Christian life and church life? Is this all God intended for His beloved people who gather in His name?

The questions that beg for answers are: Do you thirst for Him? Does your church thirst for His presence and power? Does your leadership thirst for Jesus' fullness and power in your midst? God promises, "For I will pour out water on the thirsty land / And streams on the dry ground; / I will pour out My Spirit on your offspring, / And My blessing on your descendants" (Isaiah 44:3). He freely gives grace to the humble and meets the needy who seek Him with their whole heart.

If spiritual thirst is not present, why not? The cisterns of the world from which many Christians drink never satisfy (Jeremiah 2:13). How long has it been since your church has known refreshment from heaven? How long has it been since it was like Jesus walked into your worship service revealing His presence with power? How long has it been since it was like Jesus brushed against you and you caught a fresh glimpse of His glory?

I just finished helping to lead a Prayer Conference where there was a strong sense of the Lord's revealed presence the second night. He came while we prayed and worshiped. A lady in her mid to late fifties said to me afterwards with tears, "I experienced the presence of God tonight for the first time. I can't explain what it is like. I was so broken by the Lord and His presence." A quiet teenage boy, a sophomore in high school, said to me two days later, "I experienced the presence of God for the first time Friday night, and I just cried and cried." Should this be so unusual for God's children? Our loving Father wants to reveal His presence to His children and waits for us to want it.

If we do not thirst for God in all His fullness and power then what can we do? We can ask for God to make us thirsty. He will stir us to thirst for Him if we will humbly ask with sincere desire. Persistent prayer from a needy heart is the way to the Father's heart. As a loving Father His heart is touched by His child's humble and needy cry. He gladly responds when we want Him in fullness so that we can minister His life to the needs of people. Prayer is the open mystery that allows God to work.

The Hebrides revival previously referred to came after men met night after night to pray. They knew something was lacking in their church life. With burdened souls they prayed late into the night, went to work the next day, only to return the next night to seek God again. They had such a burden from the Lord regarding the condition of their church that they could not go on with church routine as usual. They passionately wanted God to do something new among them. Every outpouring of the Holy Spirit I have read about began with people burdened to pray for God to come down in a mighty visitation of His Spirit.

Healing and restoration come to those Christians who are honest, humble and who call out to God for His intervention. Only Christ's revealed presence can bring renewal once again. Only His power can set hearts aflame and change the present state of things. If He does not, then church life will continue to be business as usual, even though it may have numerical and financial success, be doctrinally accurate, resound with enthusiastic singing, and have excellent expositional preaching. If we thirst for what God wants to give for His own glory, then the path to renewal requires that we cast off complacency and self-satisfaction, admit our spiritual poverty, humble ourselves, and doggedly pursue the God of heaven, refusing to be content with the same old comfortable and casual ways we have known so long.

Leonard Ravenhill wrote, "I offer it as my considered judgment that the main reason why we do not have heaven-born, Spirit-operated revival in our day is that WE ARE CONTENT TO LIVE

WITHOUT IT."[8] Perhaps this sums up why we do not see more of the presence and power of Jesus in our churches and our lives. For too long we have been content with business as usual and not trusted for the Spirit to manifest the resurrected Christ among us here and now. We have not taken His promises seriously, like we see in Luke 11:13, and persistently pursued our gracious Father to keep His Word. Jesus taught us by illustration (Luke 11:5–12) that there are times when we must be like the host who received the midnight visitor only to find his pantry empty. Without His Spirit filling and anointing us, we have nothing of the Lord's presence and power to offer to the hurting, the burdened, the spiritually blind, the downtrodden, or the spiritually hungry. When we are convinced that our Father will reveal Christ's presence, and that is what we most urgently need, then we will seek until we find. He promises emphatically again and again that we will find, that He will give.

The Lord's presence with power is not an everyday experience, but it should occur more often than it does in churches and individual lives. God does not want us to live on experiences, or from experience to experience. We live by faith. We trust God and believe Him for what He says. We hold to His Word even when our feelings are flat. We obey His will even when there is no inspiration. We learn to live in relationship with Him believing steadfastly what He promises and doing implicitly what He says. But even then we long to know His presence and power with us as a dynamic reality.

We have seen that the life of Jesus cannot be explained apart from the working of the Holy Spirit. Your Christian life should not be able to be explained apart from the Holy Spirit. Your church's ministry should not be able to be explained apart from the Holy Spirit. In America, Japan, and other developed countries, we have the human means to get things done. The result is that much of what happens in church life can be explained by man's ingenuity, organizational skills, plans, efforts, and methods. Although these elements are good and necessary in church life, we are too easily content to live without the disclosed presence of Jesus when this is what we truly need. It is quite true that we should know and enjoy His nearness by simple and quiet faith in our daily living. However, we terribly need those occasions when we experience the unclothed presence and power of Christ. This encourages and refreshes and energizes and renews and assures us like nothing else.

Infinite and eternal Father,

You are beautiful in holiness. You are beautiful in love. You are beautiful in humble Sovereignty. You are astounding in power. Too much do we see the things of man and this world—the lust of the eyes, the lust of the flesh, and the pride of life. Too little do we see You in Your beauty and experience Your nearness. Too much do we see what our efforts try to do and too little do we see what Your power can do. Yet, we know that what truly satisfies our soul is when You let us see Yourself.

Gracious Father, please let us see more of You than we ever have. Give us that longing to see who Your Spirit came to reveal, our Lord Jesus Christ. We need the reality of His presence with us. We need Your fullness in us. We need Your anointing upon us. Without that our pantry is empty. Lord, make us thirsty for You and then gloriously satisfy our thirst. Amen.

Notes

[1] Martyn Lloyd-Jones, *Revival*, (Westchester, Illinois: Crossway Books, 1987), 100.

[2] Duncan Campbell, *The Price and Power of Revival*, (Fort Washington, Pennsylvania: Christian Literature Crusade), 9–10.

[3] Testimony of Joseph Kemp quoted in Brian H. Edwards, *Revival! A People Saturated with God*, (Durham, England: Evangelical Press, 1990), 95.

[4] Ibid. 93–163

[5] Philip Yancey, *The Jesus I Never Knew*, (Grand Rapids, Michigan: Zondervan Publishing House, 1995), 23.

[6] Pastor Jim Cymbala's books like *Fresh Wind, Fresh Fire, Fresh Faith,* and other newer ones, recount God's powerful working in the normal life of this refreshing church.

[7] William Shakespeare, *Hamlet, Prince of Denmark,* Act IV, Scene iii, Line 9.

[8] Leonard Ravenhill, *Sodom Had No Bible,* (Zachary, Louisiana: Ravenhill Books, 1971), 11.

Conclusion

What is the essence, heart, and core of the Spirit's work today? What is the central, focal element in his many-sided ministry? Is there one basic activity to which his work of empowering, enabling, purifying, and presenting must be related in order to be fully understood? Is there a single divine strategy that unites all these facets of his life-giving action as means to one end?

I think there is, and now I offer my view of it—a view that I focus . . . in terms of the idea of presence. By this I mean that the Spirit makes known the personal presence in and with the Christian, and the church of the risen, reigning Saviour, the Jesus of history, who is the Christ of faith.

—J. I. Packer, *Keep in Step with the Spirit*

My search and experience these many years has again and again confirmed to me that our heavenly Father passionately longs to give the wondrous gifts of His Holy Spirit's fullness and the revealed presence of Jesus to all His children. He does this for His own pleasure and praise.

The preface explains why I even began this project, which was a visitation by the Holy Spirit upon missionaries and Japanese Christians in Kyoto, Japan during a seminar. Chapter 1 began with an eyewitness testimony about the first time I saw the Holy Spirit descend upon a group of people with unexpected and unexplainable results forty years ago. Since that time there have been other occasions when I have witnessed this wonderful happening.

Most recently, in October of 2004 in a local church while I was rewriting the final draft of this manuscript, I was further encouraged from God that what I had written is truly the heart of God Himself. The occasion was a Prayer Conference at Faith Evangelical Church near Chicago. Their Pastor, Dave Tipton, a former noseguard in the National Football League who played for the New England Patriots and the San Diego Chargers, invited me to come and teach them about the Person of the Holy Spirit. The conference began Friday night and was scheduled to end early Saturday afternoon. The closing session would be the Sunday morning worship service.

When I finished the last session early Saturday afternoon there was an unusual stillness—a holy quietness. I sensed I was witnessing God doing something special for this church family. Finally, there came an inner nudging within my heart to proceed with an invitation for any who wanted the Spirit's fullness to come to the elders for prayer. (Let me mention here that it is not necessary to have someone pray for you to be filled with the Spirit, but sometimes it is helpful just like with any other prayer.) I had the elders stand together to my left at the front. Because of personal illustrations I had used during the Bible teaching, I did not want the people to think it had something to do with me, but rather for them to know that it is only the Lord Jesus Christ through the power of the Holy Spirit doing what He delights to do. The Father's hand is not tightly closed as if to say, "Pry it open for My blessing if you can." Rather His hand is open and extended, waiting to give freely to His thirsty children when they yield to Him and ask in faith. I have never known humble, thirsty and surrendered believers whom God did not satisfy with the abundant fullness of His presence. Pastor Dave wrote about what happened:

As a church body we had been anticipating this conference and were expecting a touch from our Lord. The Lord had been teaching us about His presence, and we have had mercy drops before, but this year God broke through in a way that we had never seen Him do before. This weekend God gave us the gift of Himself, and we are changed. His touch came in a way that we didn't expect and with an added element of a "hands on" approach. This made it all the more precious. One of the men said that Jesus wanted to bless us by putting His hands on us and then pray over us.

For the last few months the Lord had been preparing us for this conference. We have had a growing appetite for revival, which is really just an increased thirst for God. We had been praying for more of God's Spirit to be poured out upon us, and part of that answer came during our conference. Some said that with bowed heads they had sensed His presence so powerfully they were afraid to look up. As Jerry was about to close the last session on Saturday afternoon there was a very long pause. One person told me later that they just knew during that pause that something was about to happen, and so it did! Before the last session on Saturday Jerry told me that he believed the Lord might be leading him to have those who desired the fullness of the Holy Spirit to come forward and have the Elders lay hands on them and pray for them. I did not know what to expect, and to tell you the truth, I was thinking nobody will come forward to do this and it would be an empty invitation. But God then melted us into a oneness of the Spirit that we had never known before.

One of the elders wrote, "It seemed during the conference that tears were my only appropriate response. I truly felt as though God put His arms around us and caused me to want more of Him."

Ian, a young lad about thirteen years old, came forward and laid his head on my heart as we Elders prayed for him. The next day his mother shared with us what he had said about the conference. Their family has a custom of putting an extra blanket on while tucking each other in. She said when someone else does it for you it just feels warmer. It feels like you are being loved. For Ian's family this is a way of showing each other love. Ian told his mother, "Mom, you know how we like to tuck each other in and put an extra blanket on each other? Well, when I went forward to have the Elders pray over me it was like the Holy Spirit was a blanket and the Elders were helping to put Him on me."

During our services we had a nursery for the mothers with children. As we were experiencing that touch from the Lord a mother in the meeting thought of Cara who was working in the nursery and thought she has to come up here. Carey went down to relieve Cara and told her, "You have to go up and be in that meeting. God is doing something wonderful. As Cara was coming up to the meeting she said, "I didn't know what to expect." As she walked into the room she began to weep. She said, "I knew I was walking into the presence of the Lord. You just knew it was Jesus for there was such a sense of His presence."

One young girl told me later that she almost never cries and found herself crying in the presence of the Lord Jesus. Another said she hates to hug people, but she found herself embracing one of her friends.

Another said, "When we went to lunch we were not talking about the experience. It was as if we knew what had happened and were still basking in the glow of His glory and still didn't want to touch it. Several said, "We just didn't want to go home. We didn't want it to end." One woman said, "It was like the Holy Spirit fell on us." While still another said, "It felt like when you first fall in love."

I would have to say that we all felt a genuine love for each other like we have never felt. I have never before awakened out of my sleep with sobbing, but I did that next morning. My heart was filled with thanks to God, and an unusual love for my people. I had been given a glimpse of them through the eyes of Christ. How beautiful they looked to me that next Sunday morning, and what an honor I felt in being able to serve them.

One of the members present was moved to write about what had happened that Saturday. A strong wind was blowing against the building, and we were meeting in an upstairs assembly room where we could hear the wind gusting. From this member's heart flowed these words onto a page:

> . . . And there we were, in an upper room, assembled together. The wind outside was blowing fiercely. We could hear it as it swept past, but we knew not from where it came.
>
> "I will pour out My Spirit on all people" (Acts 2:17).
>
> One by one, those who were thirsty for the fullness of His Spirit were called forward by His Spirit. And the Holy One blessed them, and called them by name . . . Just as God poured out His Holy Spirit on those in the upper room at Pentecost, who walked this earth with Him, so He pours Himself out onto those who thirst for Him today. Would He hold back? Would He give less of Himself today to the saints who love Him, to the disciples who are devoted to Him? Jesus Christ is the same yesterday and today and forever (Hebrews 13:8), pouring out His Spirit like water to sustain the thirsty ones.

. . . And we said without voice, "How can we turn ourselves over to the day—when He is here and we must go from this room?" And He whispered, "I will never leave you . . . "

Please do not withdraw Thy Spirit from my heart!
I fear, my God, it will depart
from me.
And softly You say,
"It will stay."

And the promise of Thy peace—
I fear, my Lord, that it may cease
in me.
And sweetly You say,
"It will stay."

But my hunger may subside!
I fear, my God, that I'll be earthly satisfied.
And gently You say,
"I Am Life.
I will stay.
I will never go away."

Another member recounts, "My first thought, when you called on us to come to the front of the room on that Saturday afternoon was, 'Do we do this in our congregation? Of course the answer was no. It had never been done. But once I came forward the Spirit lifted me. I was so in awe of His presence that I cannot remember anything that happened after that until the last prayer was spoken. Since then, most days when I wake up I am singing, 'Breathe on me Breath of God . . . ' It was a humbling experience that I hope to be a part of again."

Six weeks later the pastor's wife wrote, "Our dear church family is still speaking, writing down their thoughts, and also writing beautiful poetry in reflection of the conference. The Lord really touched us."

Why do we not see this more often in church life? What does our Lord want from us so that we allow Him to meet our emptiness with

His overflowing fullness and give us Christ's disclosed presence by the Holy Spirit? Why are we not more often like the New Testament Christians who greatly rejoiced "with joy inexpressible and full of glory" (1 Peter 1:8)?

Pastor Winslow addressed this issue when he wrote in the eighteen hundreds:

> The solemn conviction of the writer has long been that much of the spiritual darkness, little comfort and consolation, dwarfish piety, harassing doubts and fears, imperfect apprehensions of Jesus, the feeble faith, drooping state of the soul, and uncertainty of their full acceptance in Christ that mark so many of the professing people of God today may be traced to the absence of a deep sealing of the Spirit . . .
>
> Again we say, with all the earnestness, which a growing sense of the vastness of the blessing inspires, seek to be sealed of the Spirit; seek "the earnest of the Spirit"; seek to be "filled with the Spirit"; seek the "anointing of the Spirit"; seek the "Spirit of adoption." Do not say that it is too immense a blessing, too high an attainment for one so small, feeble, and obscure as you. Impeach not thus the grace of God. All His blessings are the bestowments of grace; grace means free favor to the most unworthy.[1]

If we want to see the glory of Christ, "glory as of the only begotten from the Father, full of grace and truth" (John 1:14), then the active work of the Holy Spirit is necessary and must be humbly sought for in our midst. This will not happen just because we know the terminology, or understand the doctrine, or speak the language of the Spirit, but this will only transpire when we persevere, persistently seeking for—with clean and humble hearts—the fullness and anointing of the Person of the Holy Spirit, the very One who animated and empowered the life of Jesus Christ.

Receiving and experiencing the fullness of the Spirit is not a quick "fix it all" for selfish reasons. The fullness of the Holy Spirit is for God's glory, honor, and praise. It is given to those who hunger and thirst for an intimate relationship with Him and long to see Jesus Christ glorified above all else. Oswald Chambers addresses this powerfully in the March 12 reading of *My Utmost for His Highest*: "Abandonment is not *for* anything at all. We have got so commercialized that we only go to God for something from Him, and not for Himself. It is like saying, 'No, Lord, I don't want You, I want myself; but I want myself clean and filled with the Holy Spirit; I want to be put in Your showroom and be able to say—"This is what God has for me."' If we only give up something to God because we want more back, there is nothing of the Holy Spirit in our abandonment; it is miserable commercial self-interest."

The fullness of God's Spirit within is indeed for every individual believer, but God also intends that it be a collective reality in the corporate body of Christ. It is necessary for believers to love one another as Jesus commanded (John 13:34–35), and thereby be strong witnesses that Christ truly transforms lives and causes them to relate differently in this world whose ways are selfish and proud (Romans 12:2). The instructions and command of Ephesians 5:18–19 address both the individual and the corporate church body, no matter which denomination. Gordon Fee, an outstanding New Testament scholar, wrote in his significant work on the Holy Spirit, "Here, perhaps, is an even greater need—that God's people collectively be so 'full of God' by His Spirit that our worship and our homes give full evidence of the Spirit's presence; by song, praise, and thanksgiving that simultaneously praise and adore God and teach the community, and by the kind of submission of ourselves to one another in which the concern is not 'who's in charge around here,' but how to love in the family as Christ loved the church and gave himself for her."[2]

Jesus' life from His conception to His enthronement cannot be explained apart from the all-powerful working of the Holy Spirit. Also there is no way the early church can be explained except in the light of the "clothing with power" from on high that Jesus promised His Father would send to all His disciples (Luke 24:49). So it should be with our Christian lives and churches. An unexplainable Christian life is one that manifests the fruit of the Spirit (Galatians 5:22–23). It is a life of humility and purity, righteousness and holiness, kindness and gentleness. Concisely, it is a life filled with Christ Himself that shows forth Divine love and grace to those it encounters everywhere: at home, at school, at work, in the grocery store, or restaurant, or wherever He leads us. It reaches out to a lost world with His truth and grace. It is what life would be like if Jesus lived it here on earth now.

Our lives and ministries and churches should be intensely real with the life and power of Jesus Christ manifested through our mortal flesh, even with all our weaknesses and quirks. We should live with awe as we regularly see Jesus be who He is and do what He alone can do in and through believers who are obedient and abandoned to Him.

How is God glorified if your life or ministry, or your church's ministry, can be explained by natural ability, or a charismatic personality, or planning skills, or anything else a human being can do? "That which is born of the flesh is flesh" (John 3:6). God is only glorified when the Spirit accomplishes the unexplainable by His Divine power, and testifies of Jesus Christ by exposing His presence. "That which is born of the Spirit is spirit" (John 3:6). Natural ability can bring the applause of men, but any heart that desires heaven's applause will seek what God alone can do. The Spirit works by shining heaven's spotlight on Christ and exalting Him, and this glorifies the Father. His works are often unexpected, they cannot be explained away, and are definitely not boring or predictable.

We were privileged to have been in China twice in the last few years where we visited house churches. In China they do not have all the expertise, money, organization, buildings, skill, and big programs that we have in America, but they do have what every church needs—the presence of God. As we met with them, there was an overwhelming sense of God's presence that brought tears even though we could not understand what was sung, prayed, or spoken, except the little that was translated for us. But when they prayed there was a deep and heartfelt calling out to God as they each voiced their prayers all at the same time. I saw those dear Chinese brothers and sisters doing in the Holy Spirit's overflow what we in America are always trying to get Christians to do through retreats, seminars, and study courses.

On a cold rainy Sunday some of us visited a rural house church that met in a warehouse-type building. Most house churches meet in small apartments. This building had concrete block walls, a concrete floor, no heat, and dim light. The benches the people sat on were nothing but narrow boards on low support posts with no backs. The people were dressed in their thick winter Chinese clothing and poverty was written all over them. We went through the service not understanding a word that was sung or spoken. At the conclusion the pastor wanted me to say something. I went to the front and turned to face the people. Our host, whom I call my Chinese son because he came to Christ through our ministry while on a business trip to the United States and has since become very dear to us, translated for me. As I looked upon their faces and saw the conditions under which they met I could not help but think of what we call church in America with our fine facilities, money, freedom, and Christian literature. I was keenly aware how we have squandered so much of God's blessings. As I faced these poor Chinese brethren who continually live with the threat of daily persecution, I was truly ashamed of what we call Christianity and church in our own country. I could not speak but instead burst into tears. After awhile I gained my composure and said to them that we needed them to pray for us. I described the conditions that we enjoy as Christians in the free world and told them that to whom much is given much is required. I admitted to them that with all we enjoy in America we have a great need. I concluded, "We need the presence of God in American churches. Please pray for us."

When I finished my Chinese son, Liu, said that they wanted to sing a song for us. The Chinese brothers and sisters stood and began to sing a song of blessing to us. With upturned faces and tears streaming down their cheeks they sang with all their hearts:

> I pray peace be with all the Lord's servants.
> May they be faithful and courageous.
> I pray the Lord's servants love one another,
> Together protect the Lord's vineyard.

I learned later that we had been the first foreigners to visit them and to this moment I am deeply moved when I remember this very humbling experience. Our team returned home more keenly aware of the lack of His presence within our American churches.

As I was writing this conclusion, several people mentioned a book written by a Chinese Christian. Brother Yun tells his story in *The Heavenly Man*. It's been said of this book that it is like "reading a modern-day version of the Book of Acts." Indeed it is. In his chapter titled "Reflecting on the West," he says:

> Before I traveled to the West I had absolutely no idea that so many churches were spiritually asleep. I presumed the Western church was strong and vibrant because it had brought the gospel to my country with such incredible faith and tenacity. Many missionaries had shown a powerful example to us by laying down their lives for the sake of Jesus.
>
> On some occasions I've struggled while speaking in Western churches. There seems to be something missing that leaves me feeling terrible inside. Many meetings are cold and lack the fire and presence of God that we have in China.
>
> In the West many Christians have an abundance of material possessions, yet they live in a backslidden state. They have silver and gold, but they don't rise up and walk in Jesus' name. In China we have no possessions to hold us down, so there's nothing preventing us from moving out for the Lord. The Chinese church is like Peter at the Beautiful Gate. When he saw the crippled beggar he said, "Silver or gold I do not have, but what I have I give you. In the name of Jesus Christ of Nazareth, walk!" Acts 3:6 . . . It's almost impossible for the church in China to go to sleep in its present situation. There's always something to keep us on the run, and it's very difficult to sleep while you're running. If persecution stops, I fear we'll become complacent and fall asleep.[3]

Brother Yun also says, "When revival came to believers in China, the result was thousands of evangelists being sent out to all corners of the nation, carrying fire from the altar of God with them. When God moves in the West, it seems you want to stop and enjoy his presence and blessings too long, and build an altar to your experiences."[4]

Our Chinese brother further points out, "Every house church pastor in China is ready to lay down his life for the gospel. When we live this way, we'll see God do great things by his grace."[5] This means that for these pastors in China personal reputation and public acclaim are not the issues but rather whatever will bring glory to God no matter the cost so that the gospel can be proclaimed.

Does this mean there has to be persecution in the West for us to experience the presence of God? Of course not! But it may come in some degree. God will meet any of His children who desperately want Him. The very serious danger we have is that all we enjoy in our freedom and prosperity will hinder what God wants to do in us. Our complacency and lack of abandonment to Him, as well as our failure to thirst for His presence in fullness, prevent us from having what we so desperately need. The solemn fact is this: The enticements and roots we put down in this world are a far greater threat to the church than persecution will ever be.

A friend who was reading Brother Yun's book asked me recently, "What would you say we lack in our country that keeps us from experiencing God's presence?" I replied with one word, "Thirst!"

In an earlier chapter I referred to L. L. Legters who wrote a little book much used by God in the Shantung revival in north China in the 1930s. V. R. Edman, a former and much respected president of Wheaton College, wrote in the foreword of the sixth edition: "The first time I heard L. L. Legters I was a young volunteer for the mission field; the last time was in Wheaton College Chapel. Both occasions, and many in between, were marked by the presence and power of God's Spirit. What he wrote in *The Simplicity of the Spirit-filled Life* was not theory to him, nor to them that heard him speak, it was a glorious reality." This kind of life glorifies God. And we can experience this spiritual reality today whether we are pastors or plumbers, missionaries or mechanics, teachers or technicians.

What a stark contrast that is with what I now share with you from a respected Christian leader of many years. I recently visited with this long-time friend, and on the way to the airport he began to speak about something I wish I could have taped. My friend has had a wide and "successful" ministry that has caused him to be well-known. I asked him if he would write down as much as he could remember of what he had said to me. This is what he sent to me:

> It can be a dangerous thing to put a Bible in the hands of a magnetic, gifted, attractive preacher. It is all too easy for him and his hearers to attribute the power of the gospel to the preacher's great ability to preach it. We even have a traditional system of recognition, which serves such an idea. Unfortunately, the word "popular" has become one of the primary measurements of a "powerful" pulpit. Our recognition vocabulary is replete with a "sanctified glossary" which only better serves the misapplication of glory. The bigger the crowd, the louder the applause, the larger the sales, the bigger the name, we can conclude as evidence of God's sanction and power. In such circumstances, the preacher can assume he has a holy effectiveness, which actually invites him to enjoy more than his share of God's spotlight. A popular preacher can easily be set up for a powerlessness to overtake him, which he does not even recognize. The gospel, which is its own power, can accomplish the purpose for which it was sent while preachers and crowds, at least in large measure, think the power of it all is found in the staging, and "the man," and in the endorsement of response.

Andrew Murray wrote, "As long as we take glory from one another, as long as we seek and love and jealously guard the glory of this life, the honor and reputation that comes from men, we do not seek and cannot receive the glory that comes from God . . . Is it any wonder that our faith is weak when pride still reigns and we have hardly learned to long or pray for humility as the most necessary and blessed part of salvation?"[6]

Murray also says, "Once again, let me repeat what I have said before. I feel deeply that we have very little concept of what the church suffers as a result of its lack of humility—the self-abasement that makes room for God to prove His power."[7]

When the Holy Spirit fills and anoints and reveals Christ through His servants, it is far beyond their natural ability. There comes an unearthly dimension—yes, heaven's Breath—upon the lives and ministries of ordinary human beings, even weak ones—especially weak ones (2 Corinthians 12:9–10)—to accomplish the unexplainable works of God.

We must be careful that we do not confuse apparent visible success and human applause with what God treasures. "He does not take pleasure in the legs of a man" (Psalm 147:10), nor does He take pleasure in any other of man's natural abilities or accomplishments. He takes pleasure in those who fear Him and wait for His lovingkindness (Psalm 147:11). He dwells with the "contrite and lowly of spirit" (Isaiah 57:15). He takes pleasure in the humble. He takes pleasure in those who have faith and trust Him out of longing hearts. He takes pleasure in a person's usefulness because of the Holy Spirit's fullness and anointing whether he is especially gifted or not.

By way of reminder, there are key words that point the way to enter the Spirit's fullness and usefulness by His power: thirsty soul, humble spirit, clear conscience, surrendered life, and receptive heart through faith. Infinitely more than you want all God has for you does He want you to enjoy all He has provided for you through the cross of Jesus, the resurrection of Christ, and the Holy Spirit at Pentecost.

With penetrating insight A. W. Tozer wrote decades ago:

> One distinguishing mark of those first Christians was a supernatural radiance that shined out from within them. The sun had come up in their hearts and its warmth and light made unnecessary any secondary sources of assurance. They had the inner witness.

It is obvious that the average evangelical Christian today is without this radiance. Instead of the inner witness we now substitute logical conclusions drawn from texts . . .

Nothing can take the place of the *touch* of God in the soul and the sense of Someone there. Where true faith is, the knowledge of God will be given as a fact of consciousness altogether apart from the conclusions of logic. The spiritual giants of old *experienced* God.

We are only now emerging from a long ice age during which an undue emphasis was laid upon objective truth at the expense of subjective experience.

Wise leaders should have known that the human heart cannot exist in a vacuum. If Christians are forbidden to enjoy the wine of the Spirit they will turn to the wine of the flesh for enjoyment . . . Christ died for our hearts and the Holy Spirit wants to come and satisfy them.[8]

Dr. Tozer also wrote, "When the Spirit presents Christ to our inner vision it has an exhilarating effect on the soul much as wine has on the body. The Spirit-filled man may literally dwell in a state of spiritual fervor amounting to a mild and pure inebriation. God dwells in a state of perpetual enthusiasm. He pursues His labors always in a fulness of holy zeal."[9]

L. L. Legters wrote in the preface to the first edition of *The Simplicity of the Spirit-filled Life*: "I have always been taught that God seeks men, not men God; but it has been only recently that I have begun to know that the great longing for Spirit-filled lives comes from the heart of God; that it is the holy God who seeks after men, who yearns and longs to fill men. The secret of being filled with the Spirit lies in letting God do for us what He most desires to do, namely to fill us."[10]

Two illustrations may help reveal the simplicity of it.

I had ordered a pair of noise-canceling headphones to use for listening to music on long airplane flights. I anticipated their arrival from a company that has a good reputation for on-time delivery by special parcel service. The day came when the package was supposed to arrive, but it hadn't come. Usually the truck driver rings the doorbell to let us know a package has arrived. There was no doorbell all day! Late in the day I decided to go on the Internet where I could track my anticipated package to see where it was and when it might arrive. I typed in the information and the following came up on my computer screen: "Package left on the front porch." I had looked through the window in the door but had not seen my package. So I went and opened the front door, and there it was leaning against the door where I could not see it. I thought, "What an interesting day we live in that I can go to my computer in the kitchen and learn that a package has arrived at my front door." All I had to do was open the door and take it into my possession. In the same way the Holy Spirit was given at Pentecost so every believer can be filled with Him and experience the reality of Christ's presence. He has already come in all His fullness. He has come even for the least one who feels most unworthy. All any Christian has to do is remove any hindrances, open up to Him, and receive this wonderful gift already delivered.

When I finished the series of meetings in Kyoto, Japan that I told about in the preface, I was very ready to return home. It had been a long and intense time. We were in an opposite time zone from where we live and because of it I was awake in the middle of the night, but also I awoke with a burden to pray for the people and the meetings. By the end of our time there, with little sleep plus speaking and counseling, I was spent and ready for rest.

We went to the airport in Osaka to catch our plane for home. When my wife Gerrie and I got to the ticket counter, the attendant looked at our tickets and said, "Mr. and Mrs. White, we are changing your seat assignment today. We are moving you into business class." I said, "Why?" She said something like, "It is a special day and we want to do this for you." I still didn't understand, and Gerrie and I looked at each other with some bewilderment. The attendant gave us our tickets with our new seat assignments, and we proceeded to the waiting area. In our weariness we were very, very thankful for this kindness, which we believe the Lord Himself arranged for us.

When we got on the huge Boeing 747-400, we were shown our seats in business class. I always wondered what went on behind those closed curtains and now I know. It would make tourist class very jealous. We took our seats in large recliner-type seats, each with its own television. We made ourselves comfortable and immediately the flight attendant came and said, "Mr. and Mrs. White, can I get you anything? If I can do anything to make your flight more comfortable, just let me know." We were served and cared for quite well just as if we had paid the thousands of dollars necessary to fly in this superb comfort for the twelve-hour flight back to the States. We had to change planes two more times to get back home and each time, much to our surprise and enjoyment, they changed our seat assignment to be in first class.

Suppose I had said to the Japanese ticket agent, "I'm sorry, but we have always flown tourist class, and we prefer the cramped seats, crowded rows, and cheaper food back there. We would rather be where we have always been." We would have still reached our destination, but it would not have been with the gracious and costly gift for the best means of travel on our long trip. So it is with our Christian journey. Our heavenly Father has offered you and me a wonderful, gracious, and costly Gift purchased by His own Son's shed blood at the cross. In addition to His unfathomable gifts of forgiveness for all our sins, a righteous standing before a holy God, the promise of eternal life in heaven, spirit union with Jesus Christ, and the glorious reality of adoption whereby God is actually your heavenly Father, He offers you the gift of His Spirit's fullness and the manifested presence of Jesus Christ. What will you do with these gifts He offers? Will you continue your Christian journey while refusing His wondrous gifts of the Holy Spirit's fullness, and the energizing that comes by the revealed presence of Jesus Christ, or will you enjoy to the fullest His astonishing grace? Through your faith in Jesus Christ you will reach heaven, but unless you receive all Jesus purchased for you by His costly and loving sacrifice, your journey will be far less than your Father has offered to you and longs to give to you. He fully knows your unworthiness, and does not require that you be perfect or fully mature or walk without stumbling. For His own unfathomable reason He wants to lavishly pour upon you His steadfast and infinite grace with all its attending gifts.

It is your Father's good pleasure to give all of His wondrous gifts to you so that your life will bring Him praise, honor, and glory.

Beautiful Lord,

Your humility equals Your majesty.
Your purity is as regal as Your sovereignty.
O matchless One,
When one beholds Your beauty—
Adoring silence is the only fitting and first response.
Then suddenly worship gushes from the wellspring
of Your Life within me, and with angelic beings
I cry, "HOLY! HOLY! HOLY!"
All glory, majesty, dominion, authority, and praise
Before all time and now and forever belong to You.
Amen!

Notes

[1] Winslow, *Morning Thoughts*, 766–767. Other men like the Puritan Thomas Goodwin and the great London pastor, Dr. Martyn Lloyd-Jones, call an extraordinary encounter with the Holy Spirit the *sealing with the Spirit*. They think of it as an experience subsequent to salvation. Others pre-dating Pentecostalism and the Charismatic emphasis called it *the baptism of the Spirit*. Pastor Winslow seems to group all these terms together to drive home the point that what we need is the reality, experience, and fullness of the Holy Spirit in our lives. I personally disagree with the term *sealing of the Spirit* and *baptism of the Spirit* referring to an experience subsequent to salvation, but I understand the urgent note Pastor Winslow is sounding. *Sealing with the Spirit* occurs at conversion and is not necessarily experiential. God *seals believers with the Holy Spirit* through the Holy Spirit indwelling them at their conversion and from that moment on they are stamped as God's own property.

[2] Gordon Fee, *God's Empowering Presence*, (Peabody Massachusetts: Hendrickson Publishers, Inc., 1994), 722.

[3] Brother Yun with Paul Hattaway, *The Heavenly Man*, (Mill Hill, London & Grand Rapids, Michigan: Monarch Books, 2002), 295–296.

[4] Ibid., 296.

[5] Ibid., 300.

[6] Murray, *Humility*, 78.

[7] Ibid., 57.

[8] A. W. Tozer, *Gems from Tozer, Selections from the Writings of A. W. Tozer*, (Bromley, Kent, England: Send the Light Trust, 1969), 18–19.

[9] Ibid., 31.

[10] Legters, *The Simplicity of the Spirit-filled Life*, 5.

Study Guide

Study Questions for Chapter One
Searching for Fullness

1. Describe a time when you witnessed God's Spirit manifest the presence of Jesus to a group. Where were you? What was it like? How did it affect you?

2. Have you ever thought something like, "There must be more to the Christian life and church life than I have known"?

3. How do you define spiritual hunger and thirst? What evidences of spiritual thirst are in your life?

4. How do you respond when you think of the Holy Spirit and His ministry? Confused? Fearful? Suspicious? Bewildered? Ignorant? Comfortable? Why?

5. Define what you think it means to be Spirit-filled.

6. Do you consider yourself to be Spirit-filled? If yes, recount how the Spirit's fullness entered your life and what the results were. If not, then why not? What is holding you back from yielding all to the Holy Spirit's control?

7. What evidence do you think a Spirit-filled life should project?

8. Have you known someone whom you knew to be Spirit-filled? What qualities did you see in his or her life?

9. Do you equate the filling of the Spirit with some dramatic experience? If so, what kind of experience?

10. Describe how important you think the Spirit's fullness is for the Christian life.

Study Questions for Chapter Two
Another Helper Like Jesus

1. What evidence do we consistently see through the Old Testament about the Holy Spirit?

2. What is significant about the Holy Spirit in Jesus' life?

3. Do you think that evangelical Christians see the importance of the Holy Spirit as Jesus emphasized it in Luke 24:49 and Acts 1:8? Do you?

4. Do you view the Holy Spirit as a real living Person? The third Person of the Trinity? Do you understand Him to be exactly like Jesus?

5. What are the various words that can help us understand the Greek word for *Helper*?

6. Where does the Holy Spirit dwell in relationship with the believer (John 14:17)?

7. What should the truths about the Holy Spirit revealed in John 14:17 mean for your life? How should these truths influence the way you think and behave?

8. What is the purpose of the Spirit's ministry (John 15:26, 16:14)? (Note J. I. Packer's illustration.)

9. What are a few of the Holy Spirit's ministries to and for the believer? What are His ministries through the believer?

10. What two fundamental issues must be settled in your heart if you are to enjoy your relationship with God and have peace and joy in your heart?

11. Describe your love relationship with the Lord. How is it expressed in your life everyday?

Study Questions for Chapter Three
The Spirit Comes in Fullness

1. Do you believe A. W. Tozer's quote in the epigraph to be true? Explain your answer.

2. How did the Holy Spirit poured out at Pentecost affect the first-century disciples long-term?

3. Do you see your church emphasizing the necessity of the Holy Spirit's fullness for every believer like the early church emphasized it? Explain your answer.

4. If Saul of Tarsus came to your church as a new convert, how and what would your church pray for him? Would the prayer include that he be filled with the Holy Spirit?

5. What was the significance of the Holy Spirit coming upon the Samaritans and Gentiles like He did the Jews at Pentecost?

6. If the Apostle Paul could visit your church today, do you think he would see the Holy Spirit's presence and power in the same measure as he did in his own time? Explain your answer.

7. List the four clear observations about the Holy Spirit's fullness in believers that we see in the book of Acts.

8. What is the difference between *filled* and *full* regarding believers and the Holy Spirit?

9. Write in your own words what it means to be full of the Holy Spirit.

10. What is the opposite of being full of the Holy Spirit? How is it expressed?

11. Answer the questions listed at the end of Chapter 3.

Study Questions for Chapter Four
The Way to Receive Fullness

1. Have you ever considered that God is longing to fill you with His Holy Spirit? What does such a wonderful thought mean to you?

2. Outline the path to fullness by the Holy Spirit as found in John 7:37–39.

3. What does it mean to thirst? How is spiritual thirst manifested in your life?

4. What prevents Christians from truly thirsting for God as expressed in Psalm 42:1–2 and 63:1–5? What hinders you from thirsting for God above all else?

5. How do you practically come to Christ today when He is not present physically?

6. Drinking is synonymous with _____. How do you drink of the living water of God's Spirit?

7. What is significant about the verbs in John 7:37–39?

8. What are the issues that can hinder you from being filled with the Holy Spirit? Are there any hindrances in your life? If so, what are they?

9. What is conscience and why is it so important for your life?

10. How do you clear your conscience before God and man?

11. What does it mean to steadfastly trust God and not doubt Him (James 1:6, Mark 11:24)?

12. According to Legters, what is the evidence that you are truly filled with the Spirit?

Study Questions for Chapter Five
The Way to Continue in Fullness

1. What are the key lessons we learn from John 15:1–11 about the necessity of abiding in Christ?

2. What has been your experience regarding the love of God? How is His love real to you?

3. How should our experience of God's love for us affect our love for others?

4. How does it affect you to consider that God wants an intimate, close relationship with you (James 4:8)? What are you doing so you can have this right relationship with Him?

5. What is the difference between discipline and legalism? Why do we confuse the two? How important is discipline for the Christian life?

6. Using the four seasons of the year, which one describes your intimacy with God and why?

7. What do you think it means to gaze on the Lord (2 Corinthians 3:18, Matthew 5:8)? How does someone gaze on the Lord? How do you?

8. What truths should anchor our souls to Him when we walk through pain and sorrow?

9. What helps you to remember that all of your life here on earth should be lived with eternity in view?

10. How useful to God is a life that is not filled with the Holy Spirit?

Study Questions for Chapter Six
In Step with the Spirit

1. Do you think God's Spirit directs Christians today like He did in New Testament days (Acts 16:6–7)? Explain your answer.

2. What is the main point from J. Oswald Sanders' illustration about White Fang?

3. What does it mean to quench the Spirit (1 Thessalonians 5:19)?

4. What is the difference between living by the Law and living by the Spirit?

5. What are three guiding principles for staying in step with the Spirit?

6. What must the Holy Spirit show us in addition to revealing God's truth to our hearts? According to Colossians 1:9, what is spiritual wisdom?

7. Is there something that God's Spirit has recently shown you to do to walk out His truth?

8. What evidences are there in your life that you are living by the Spirit's supernatural power?

9. How does God's direction in your life relate to your own personal planning? In the day-to-day scheme of things, how does God's direction influence the way you plan your life and the use of your time?

10. Was there a time when you planned your way but the Lord then redirected your steps? Also, tell of a time when you obeyed an inner prompting and it proved to be the will of God because the Spirit led you.

Study Questions for Chapter Seven
Exceptional Fillings by the Spirit

1. Why do you think we do not see more exceptional fillings by the Spirit in our day?

2. What is the difference between the Holy Spirit filling a believer and the Spirit of God upon a believer?

3. Explain what happened to Jesus at His baptism when the Holy Spirit came upon Him in light of the fact that He was always filled with the Spirit without measure.

4. How do you obtain the exceptional filling (anointing) of the Holy Spirit?

5. Why is pride so terrible an enemy to believers and God's work?

6. How and where does pride express its ugliness in our lives?

7. What is humility and why is it so exceedingly important for Christians? And to God?

8. Why are more Christians not like the host of the midnight visitor in Luke 11:5–8?

9. Why should we keep on asking for the Holy Spirit as Jesus taught us in Luke 11:9–13?

10. What keeps evangelical churches from experiencing the spontaneity of the Holy Spirit's control? Do you allow the Holy Spirit to have freedom in your life so that you are free to be spontaneous with obedience to His inner promptings?

Study Guide Chapter Eight
Jesus' Presence Revealed

1. What is the difference between the presence of Jesus with His disciples on earth and His presence with them after He went to heaven?

2. Describe what is evident when the Holy Spirit reveals the presence of Jesus.

3. Do you consider that God's people are distinguished today by the real presence of Christ in their midst? Explain your answer.

4. Explain how you respond to the thought that Jesus' presence can be extremely real to you and your church, even almost tangibly present?

5. What are some things that prevent us from experiencing Christ's revealed presence?

6. What is so critical about quenching the Spirit as Dr. J. I. Packer explains it?

7. How do we humble ourselves before the Lord and draw near to Him?

8. How would you describe your desire to diligently pursue God in order to know His presence?

9.   What were some of the characteristics of those times when the Spirit of God revealed Christ's presence to others?

10.   Do you believe you and your church can experience the revealed presence of Jesus? Explain the "why" of your answer.

Study Questions for Chapter Nine
The Power of Jesus' Presence

1.   If Jesus' power is the same yesterday, today, and forever, why do we not see more evidence of His power at work in our churches today?

2.   Have you ever been where Jesus' power was revealed doing the unexplainable and unexpected? If yes, describe it and tell what happened.

3.   From this chapter, how do you now understand the nature of true revival?

4.   How would you describe your church's present spiritual condition in the light of Brian Edwards' list from his book *Revival*?

5. If following Jesus was an awe-inspiring adventure for the first disciples, should it not be for us also? How do you and the Christians you know view what it is like to follow Christ?

6. How does it affect you to read eyewitness accounts of when the Holy Spirit revealed the presence of Jesus with power?

7. Tell of a time when you saw Jesus touch someone miraculously so that your faith was encouraged. Do you believe His powerful works are real and for today?

8. Describe your thirst and your church's thirst for the dynamic revelation of the presence of Jesus.

9. Why do many Christians not truly thirst for Christ's presence?

10. Why do we not have true revival according to Leonard Ravenhill?

Study Questions for the Conclusion

1. According to J. I. Packer, what is the core of the Spirit's work?

2. What is required from us if we will see the glory of Christ in our midst?

3. Why is the fullness of the Holy Spirit as important for church-life as it is for an individual Christian?

4. Is there anything about your life and your church that is unexplainable because the Holy Spirit is working with power?

5. What is your response to what my friend wrote about the magnetic, gifted, and attractive preacher?

6. Do you think God is concerned about our visible success in the eyes of men? Why do many churches put such emphasis upon it? Explain your answers.

7. What are key words that point the way to the Spirit's fullness so we can then become useful by His power?

8. If a fellow believer wanted to know how to be filled with God's Spirit, how would you instruct him or her so he or she could enter into the Spirit's fullness?

9. A clear, firm grasp of Bible truth and doctrine is hugely important. However, do you think God looks first at what we think and believe or at a heart that is hungry for His gracious fullness and wonderful presence?

10. Have you entered into the fullness of God's Holy Spirit? Do you know how to abide there?

For Further Reading

Spirit-Filled Life

Baptism & Fullness, John R. W. Stott, InterVarsity Press.

How to be Filled with the Holy Spirit, A. W. Tozer, Christian Publications, Inc. (Out of print but may be found in used book lists).

Joy Unspeakable, Martyn Lloyd-Jones, Harold Shaw Publishers.

Keep in Step with the Spirit, J. I. Packer, Fleming H. Revell Company.

The Sovereign Spirit, Martyn Lloyd–Jones, Harold Shaw Publishers.

The Spirit of Christ, Andrew Murray, Oliphants LTD (Out of print but may be found in used book lists).

Discipline and Devotion

Abide in Christ, Andrew Murray, Whitaker House Publisher or Christian Literature Crusade.

Enjoying Intimacy with God, J. Oswald Sanders, Discovery House Publishers.

Fellowship with God, Jerald R. White, Jr.; order from:
barnabasbooks@bellsouth.net.

The Spirit of the Disciplines, Dallas Willard, HarperCollins Publishers.

Spiritual Disciplines for the Christian Life, Donald Whitney, NavPress.

Through the Looking Glass, Kris Lundgaard, P & R Publishing.

Revival

Revival, Martyn Lloyd-Jones, Crossway Books.

Revival! A People Saturated with God, Brian H. Edwards, Evangelical Press.

The Heavenly Man, Brother Yun with Paul Hattaway, Monarch Books.

Printed in the United States
135517LV00001B/4/A

9 781597 813242